Heartspace

Real Life Stories on Death and Dying

Edited by

Cathy Brooks Edwards

A heart2heart Publication
Pittsboro, North Carolina
2019

First edition published for All Souls Day, November 2, 2019.

ISBN: 9781691226290

Published by heart2heart, a non-profit operating within Abundance NC, non-profit #20-4327530, on the KDP.com printing platform

Funding for this project was made available through heart2heart, and all net proceeds from the sale of this book will go to fund future heart2heart programs and projects.

heart2heart/Abundance NC
PO Box 5
Pittsboro, NC 27312

www.heart2heartnc.com

Front cover art by Andrea Saccone Snyder.
Designed for heart2heart.
www.flowgirldesigns.weebly.com

Heartspace

Real Life Stories on Death and Dying

Dedication

*To all the beloved men in my life
beginning with my father
who now guide me from beyond.*

Table of Contents

Foreword

We live in a death-phobic culture. We tend to walk backwards into death, backwards and in denial of our own mortality.

The medical industry works miracles yet too often lengthens the dying process, while quality of life declines. Often, there is another procedure or experimental drug to try, both, attempts to keep the body going. But at what cost? Half of what we spend on all health-related services is spent in the last six months of life.

As we age and die, we Baby Boomers—the Grey Tsunami—are threatening to consume a disproportionate share of our limited medical resources. All because we have a poor understanding of death. All because of how we've come to relate to death. It's time to think again about death. It's time to change how we relate to death. But how do we start?

We start by talking about death. We start by sharing our death stories. We start with this book.

This book is born out of a series of events that began when Chris Lucash, Alisa Esposito, and their three children relocated to Chatham County so Chris, who was struggling with ALS, could be close to Duke's medical facilities. They settled next to Tami Schwerin and Lyle Estill.

Shortly thereafter, in a chance encounter, Cathy Edwards and her children met Chris and Alisa's family, for an afternoon swim, on Tami and Lyle's property. Though I did not know Cathy then, I know her story now.

A friendship began between Chris and Alisa's children and Cathy's. Cathy, a licensed bodywork therapist and professional counselor, began to offer weekly hands-on-healing work to Chris along with live sacred music by local musicians, Amy Durso and John Westmoreland. Slowly, it evolved into family support work; bringing the children into the dying process through creative endeavors; providing gentle guidance; then bringing support and ritual into Chris's bedroom with his family and extended community.

In 2015, in support of Chris and his family, while Chris was in his dying time, Abundance NC, Sparkroot Farm, and the Fenwick Foundation brought Stephen Jenkinson, author of *Die Wise*, to town for a weekend workshop on death. The workshop was well attended—we were hungry for the conversation, hungry for something all-but-forgotten in these *modern* times. With Stephen's help we started talking about death, and about the unseen, and the far-reaching consequence of "how we die, how we tend to our dying, and how we carry our Dead."

It changed my life and set me on the path that has me writing these words. It was at this workshop that I first met Cathy Brooksie Edwards.

In the spring of 2016 as Chris's death neared, Tami Schwerin and Lyle Estill received the knock on the door that every parent dreads: their son Zafer had died.

At the time, I knew Tami, but not well; I was a fan and supporter of her work at Abundance NC. Zafer's death brought us closer, as loss sometimes does, and she is now a good, good friend.

Six weeks later, in June, Chris passed away. Cathy and Leif Diamant, an ordained minister, led the home funeral services for Chris.

In the fall of 2016, in the wake of these two village-tended deaths, Abundance NC held its first Death Faire.

An award-winning documentary film, *Staring Down Fate*, was released, covering Chris's life, his work with endangered wolves, his struggle with ALS, his dying time and green burial.

In the spring of 2017, Cathy and Alisa traveled to Maui to the first International Death Doula training with Doorway into Light. Since then they've developed programs such as Death and Cupcakes, a healing center, and a community green burial ground. Cathy has carried on her studies in workshops with experienced leaders in the death and dying field.

In the fall of 2018, Cathy, with the support of the Fenwick Foundation, Sparkroot Farm, and Abundance NC, founded *heart2heart*, a non-profit program, providing holistic services for living and dying.

I have personally experienced Cathy's hands-on-healing work and felt the power that comes from bathing in live music while in Cathy's care. It's a beautiful and soothing combination of sound and touch.

*****

With these two men passing, the reality of hard, untimely endings was brought front and center and wrought fully upon us. These deaths pulled us together, powerfully. They steeped us in love.

As a community we held the two families, we held each other, and shared the grief. We orchestrated two home funerals and vigils; bringing death back into our living rooms; taking care of the bodies and burials ourselves; digging the graves ourselves; lowering the pine caskets into the ground ourselves; facing and embracing death the way our great-grandparents did.

It was hard. It was healing. And it changed us.

*****

From Zafer's and Chris's deaths, and dying times that followed, this book emerges—with personal stories about death and dying.

With these stories we make our claim. We turn around and walk forward into death. As a community we walk together with hearts wide open. We set fear aside and embrace death as a natural transition—an important part of living. We share our grief and in so doing change how we live.

I am a proud supporter of *heart2heart*; of Cathy Edwards's work with the dying; of the ongoing Abundance NC and Sparkroot Farm events; and now the release of this moving anthology.

Frank J. Phoenix
October 1, 2019

Frank J. Phoenix is the president and co-founder of the Fenwick Foundation, a small family foundation supporting the evolution of culture and consciousness. He often says our challenges are not biological but rather cultural in nature, and that our challenges—our ways of being in the world, our systems of thinking, our institutions have deep roots in our culture, and that solutions emerge as we examine and change our beliefs and thus change our culture. Prior to his work with the foundation he worked as an Environmental Engineer measuring air pollution from large industrial operations. Frank lives and works in Chapel Hill, North Carolina with his wife of 45 years; together they have two beautiful children, all living and working in the Washington, DC area.

Preface

I've always been a keeper of stories.

As long as I can remember.

It started at home. Then with friends. The more people I met, the more stories I kept. They accumulated like treasured books on a shelf.

I listened, helping people make sense of their stories, holding their stories safe while they freed themselves of the weight.

Story-keeping became my profession—I trained to be a licensed counselor. Listening, listening, listening. Holding. Clarifying. Helping.

I began to see that the story we could speak was only *part* of the story.

Bodywork therapy training came next. I became a professional massage and bodywork therapist. Then I added Reiki training, hands-on-healing and Asian healing modalities. It may have looked like I was straying from my vocation as a story keeper—but it really was a deepening.

I was listening for, watching, and carrying the stories held in our bodies, drawing the connections between our spoken stories and our unspoken ones. The raised shoulders. The pain in the left forearm. The shortened breath and lack of eye contact. A slump when standing.

As the work continued, I would weave the spoken stories with the body stories for deeper insight. I helped explore the logic of the stories, the truths, the distortions of the truth, the choice of stories we tell ourselves, the possibility of changing our story.

*****

How did I come to be gathering and offering a collection of dying time stories?

It was four years ago, 2015, in Chatham County, North Carolina, that I landed in someone's dying time.

With my experience in counseling, bodywork and sacred sound, I was equipped. Equipped to be present. To witness. To honor. To facilitate those moments we fear most. To comfort the dying and those who will survive the dying time.

Our local community had been exploring dying time, death, the culture of death, and green, alternative burials.

As we went deeper into being a sustainable community, I went deeper, training as a death doula, working with hospice, helping families, and tending to the dying.

The first dying time was a spouse diagnosed with ALS. Then, a beloved son of a friend, who overdosed. A year later, another spouse. Then, a father and a grandfather. Later still, a treasured friend.

I can't tell you the moment it happened, but as the days went by it became increasingly clear to me that my work with the dying was not random, not just chance, not a casual change in direction. I could see and feel and know that working with the dying is *my* work, work I have spent my whole life preparing for, as you will learn in the prologue.

As I witnessed the stories of others who were deeply affected by the loss of their beloveds, I saw my own life story come full circle. Working with the dying, and those who survive the dying time, is my true purpose.

Along with this clarity came recognition of the power in telling our stories, and the deep healing that comes when others bear witness.

Maya Angelou said, "There is no greater agony than bearing an untold story inside of you." Through the dying times of the last four years, I came to know that.

So how did I come to *this* anthology?

It came as a thought, a whisper from the trees, a song in the wind on a mild, yet crisp, morning in January 2019.

Gather our stories and share them.

I took a breath.

I waited.

And waited.

And waited.

Then, the project took on a life of its own.

This was the birth of *Heartspace: Real Life Stories on Death and Dying*

Cathy Brooks Edwards
November 2, 2019

Introduction

First, let's say what this book is not.

It is not about the way America treats death or how we live in death-phobic times. It is not about the forgotten ancient rituals, spiritual beliefs or confronting our own mortality. It is not about how to be a death doula or guide people through the grief process.

This book is simply stories—stories told in prose and poetry, real life honest stories, raw and ragged stories, the stories of everyday people trying to make sense of death and the heavy grief it brings.

The contributors to *Heartspace: Real Life Stories on Death and Dying* invite you into their living rooms, bedrooms, kitchens, front porches, gardens, funerals and grave sites. They invite you into their hearts—their heartspace—as they share their most intimate and honest experience.

You will read stories by mothers and fathers who have buried their children after losing them to drug overdoses, miscarriages and accidents. Children who have lost their parents to horrible diseases, aging, and suicide. Sisters and brothers who struggle to let their beloved siblings go. A niece and nephew who mourn their favorite aunt. Spouses who have supported their partners through the dying time. Friends who mourn the loss of friends. A young woman who sat vigil for her grandmother in the hills of North Carolina.

The storytellers are friends and acquaintances, old and new. They come from many walks of life, different cultures, ethnicities, education, life experiences, and professions. I have known most of them for many years; a few were sent to me through trusted friends because their stories needed to be shared.

Most of the writers are from my present life in Chatham County, North Carolina—many who have shared and held the community's losses—Tami Schwerin, community weaver and cultural changemaker; Lyle Estill, author and entrepreneur; Gary Phillips, poet and amateur botanist; Carol Hewitt, author and sustainability guru; Mike Wiley, actor and playwright; Camille Armantrout, blogger and gardener; Hannah Eck, storyteller and community artisan; Barbara Viola Ford, office manager and nature lover; Sharon Blessum, shamanic practitioner and creative intuitive; Edwin Nothnagel, healer and truth-seeker; Dori DeJong, grief workshop facilitator and author; and, Leif Diamant, psychotherapist and minister.

Three inspiring women were referred to me by close friends—Karen Howard, former attorney and local county commissioner; Angela Belcher Epps, fiction and non-fiction author; and Jaki Shelton Green, state poet laureate and educator.

Far across state lines are my oldest friends—Amy Parker, child psychologist and mindfulness teacher; Diane Fine, artist and art professor; Jennifer Scanlon, biographer and women's studies professor; and Amiel Landor, clairvoyant and holistic coach—friends who have held me through some of my toughest times; heard and witnessed my losses, and kept them close to their hearts.

These tales weave a tapestry of real and honest life experiences with death and dying.

The power of storytelling is at the heart of this book. It is a channel for working with the intense emotions during dying time and the death of a beloved. Taking the risk to tell our most personal stories opens our heartspace—the container, the vessel for our most intimate, deep stories—connecting us with others.

As a reader, you are bearing witness to the feelings of sadness, anger, fear, loneliness, denial and grief that accompany death. There is healing in bearing witness to a person's story. It is a place of honor—vital in therapeutic recovery from trauma.

Digest these stories slowly. Find a soft and comfy place to sit; prepare a cup of hot tea or a shot of whiskey; and grab a box of tissues or a hankie. Read them aloud to yourself, a friend or a group of beloveds. Let them break you open and release your own sorrows. Notice your thoughts, your emotions and your body's responses. Maybe you'll want a pen and paper to write down what comes up for you, or if your heart is too heavy, ask for help.

Stories matter.

Cathy Brooks Edwards

Prologue

Spring 1969

A black rotary phone sits on the metal side table next to the wooden bench lining the long hallway.

The phone rings. I answer it with anticipation. Out of the corner of my eye, I see Mom standing down the hall.

It's Dad. He no longer lives with us.

We talk. I am guarded.

Soon it's time to wind down our call.

"I love you," Dad says.

I glance up. Mom is still there.

I pause. Mumble something about having to go. Stuff my wish to respond. Put the receiver down.

I look up. Mom has already slipped away; off into another room of our middleclass ranch house nestled in a suburban neighborhood somewhere in the Midwest.

I go about my day.

*****

The next morning. At school.

I am pulled from my second period junior high history class. Told I am going to the principal's office. I am not surprised. It isn't my first visit.

But this time, Mom is there.

I see our priest, and the principal. All standing inside the office. Waiting for me. Watching me.

Everything goes quiet.

I hear the words, "Your father is dead. He took his own life."

*****

That night.

I accompanied Mom to a friend's house.

I found my first bottle of rum, slipped into the basement alone, and tried to drink away the guilt.

*****

For years following my father's suicide I went searching for meaning, for what to do with the deep discomfort I was carrying.

My mother was carrying her own sorrow. I had no community to guide me through those uncharted waters. No one led me into the natural world, or showed me that sadness, anger and loss could be channeled into creative endeavors. No wise elders. An occasional counselor who had their own undigested material. It was just me and grief.

It didn't stop me from reaching for and achieving goals, but I was never without the profound unhappiness. I felt overwhelmed as if I were weighed down with a thick, oversized, wet wool coat. My anger came out sideways with at-risk behaviors, while sadness and sorrow filled my soul.

Winter 2018

I stand over a freshly dug hole; five feet deep and six feet long.

Dirt is piled next to one edge with shovels waiting. Soon the mourners will come.

A pool of water lingers in the bottom of the grave where a body is to be lowered in less than one hour.

It doesn't feel right. The water in a resting place. It doesn't feel respectful to place the father of children, the brother of siblings, the son of loving parents and a friend of many into a muddy hole, especially since this man will be arriving cloaked in a shroud; no simple cedar box, just a simple unadorned burial swaddling.

My mind works rapidly.

I quickly drive to the garden. Load several bales of hay. Drive back. Throw the bales into the water at the bottom of the grave. I look around the forest grounds of our cemetery for fallen trees to place as slats on top of the straw for his body to rest upon.

Now I'm on my knees, reaching down into this open cradle of earth placing the small fallen trees that will support the cycle of life and death for this man whom I have never met.

Tami arrives with fresh pink camellias, winter blossoms from her garden. She tosses them in.

*****

Now the earth is prepared. It is time for prayer. Time to acknowledge the forest that surrounds us. Time to honor the earth, the trees, the plants, the land. Time to pray to our ancestors. Our unseen guides. The many teachers who have come before us.

I light a stick of santo palo wood—a sacred wood. Time to bless the land that holds the most precious beloveds of three other families.

Silently I offer gratitude and appreciation for all the elements; the earth, the air, the fire, the water; the north, the south, the east and the west; the sky above and the earth below.

I ask for guidance to know my own path. That I may continue to be in service to my own heart, the hearts of my close beloveds, my community and the hearts of the collective.

I honor my own unseen guides and teachers by lighting a mapacho, sacred tobacco for protection, and by holding a steady heartbeat on my buffalo skin death drum.

The air crackles with the loud sound of tires on the gravel. Sunlight is softly filling the forest. The hearse pulls into the driveway.

I pause.

I have helped prepare the grave. I have helped prepare the land. I have offered gratitude. I have called upon the spirits who guide us, and, I have called upon all that is.

Now my work is to be present for the grieving family; to hold a steady and conscious space for them; to be a quiet guide; to lead the way for others to grieve and to mourn.

Slowly, I walk towards the sorrow.

Cathy Brooks Edwards

Stitching the Seams of Loss

Angela Belcher Epps

Odessa, four months gone

It's June 2015, four months since my mother's funeral. For two days I've been in her house in Plymouth, North Carolina, and it's as if my being is engulfed by her energy. This morning, as I lie in bed contemplating what this post-death day will bring, I can almost hear the rhythmic scrape of Odessa's hard-bottomed slippers making her way from bedroom to kitchen. I imagine her raising the shades, unlocking the backdoor, opening the refrigerator to pour her daily glass of juice. I rise and go to the kitchen. After I've scooped coffee from the canister, I imagine she says, "You're finished with it now, so put it back." I comply.

Until the end, Mom made a large mug of coffee and two meals a day. She remained faithful to Willing Workers meetings, weekly shopping excursions, and Sunday school at Lily of the Valley Baptist Church. She hid her true diagnosis from us and made peace with the need for night-time oxygen. Over the course of a year, she began to step a little slower and cough in longer spells, so I drove the two hours more often—to chat, catch up, keep her company. When I tried to cook extra meals, Mom balked and sulked. I'd veered out of our established roles. She was the director; I, the directed. As her pounds slowly melted, she kept the sewing machine up and ready to bring in seams of blouses, pants, and jackets. As her airways narrowed, her strongest complaint was, "I seem to be getting short of breath." But Mom continued to sweep dust and pine needles from her driveway and porches. I did as much as she'd allow and worried around the edges of her still active life.

My mother built this house for her retirement years. My mission is to hunker down in here and sift through her belongings, get my bearings as a grown woman whose mother is now in spirit. I have no immediate intention to purge or reorganize figurines and souvenirs, Tupperware and cast iron, baskets of fabric and sewing notions. Her drawers and cabinets explode with decades of cottons, silks, and wool—arranged reminders of trends ranging from the neon piqué of the 1960s to the soothing sweats and flannels of her last winter. I know her pantries and closets as surely as I know my own. Understand her passion for negotiating issues of space and logistics—like fitting ten pairs of bedroom shoes in a small plastic container beneath her bed or squeezing dozens of rolled towels into the shelves to accommodate potential housefuls of visiting relatives. I open drawers and close them. Move to the next room and get lost in turning the pages of photo albums, peering at entries in her financial ledger, reading doctor's comments from recent office visits—activities that lead to nothing more than a mind filled with details of her life.

Familiarity with Mom's ways allows me to wear my grief like a loose and gauzy garment. Something barely there, but that covers me just the same. To know someone so intimately says we were together, that we were close in spite of our differences. I feel assured to the core that I'm my mother's daughter in spite of a lifetime of her chastisements that pricked me like thorns and tightened my throat.

Mom once said in passing, "People always talk about loving a child. But the important thing is that you raise them. You've got to raise them, or they won't know how to live." At the time, her harsh take stunned and stung me. But now that she's gone, I realize her parenting perspective and practices *were* her loving gestures towards me. Her *raising* was a steady and annoying perpetuation of personal maxims to make me fit for this life:

- Put it back where you got it from.
- Clean as you cook.
- Don't want everything you see.
- Think before buying something you already have.
- Keep some money saved.
- Finish what you start and pay attention as you do it.
- Relax and put your feet up after working hard.
- Get a routine.

As I reflect during these surreal days of adjusting, I'm proud to know how to do it Odessa's way. That if her spirit watches me moving around her rooms, she nods her approval, sees evidence that I listened, learned, and now value the things that were important to her. Hope she's aware that *I* know I'm so much better off because of what she knew to give me. Which raises the question of how I'll fare without her salt-of-the-earth input when the need for such arises.

In the Midst of Moving Forward

Transforming my mother's space into a place that both feeds my soul and honors her memory will only happen this one time. Every task becomes a meditation on WWOD? (What Would Odessa Do?) It helps that holding on and reaching back didn't sit well with Mom. Mere months before her death, I retrieved her own mother's crippled oak table from a yard sale. As I struggled to get it into her shed, Mom asked, "Why are you keeping this broken table?"

"It's your mother's. It was Mama's. From probably sixty years ago. At least."

Mom rolled her eyes. "So what? What are you gonna do with it?"

Yet I grapple with what it means to relinquish her earthly possessions. Her things still seem to be hers. When I bring random pots and linens back to my home in Raleigh, I harbor a bit of guilt—as if I've taken her belongings without permission. These unsettling sentiments nudge me to slow down and line up with new truths. For instance, dead mothers have no further need for their acquisitions. Removing her robe from the hook behind her bedroom door symbolizes nothing.

I relax alone with a glass of wine at the end of a day comprised solely of pulling out and contemplating hundreds of items. I remember Mom's busy-ness after each of her three younger sisters' deaths. She led me and her remaining sisters through these tasks, last rites—

sharing anecdotes and laughing as we emptied closets, separated keepsakes from trash, swept and mopped their floors for the last time. Mom took dry-eyed cigarette and coffee breaks, modeling for us how to approach death as sensible and capable survivors. To grieve the dead without flinching—letting sweat be the salty liquid shed in response to loss.

Renewal, renovation, and restoration resided in Mom's soul. Knowing this extends her strength and common sense to me. Makes it easier to release yards and yards of fabric I'll never use. To paint over nicotine-yellowed walls—reminders of her unapologetic commitment to cigarettes—with hot pink and teal. I invite her cousins and friends to come by and take what they want with a clear conscience.

Still, as I proceed, I look for signs that it's okay to keep going. I set up an altar with items that capture her spirit: candle holders, the cast iron skillet passed down from her mother, pin cushions, small tools, a jar of her annual fig preserves, rolled coins, her frayed wallet that never ran out of cash, a cigarette case and lighter, motivating plaques that graced her kitchen walls. Whenever I arrive, I light a candle in gratitude for all she's done for me, then have my way in her home.

Four Years Gone

Often when I go to Plymouth which is now my getaway, Mom's sister witnesses me in action—putting on pots to simmer, tackling a sewing project with deft fingers, weeding Mom's flowerbeds for hours. She'll say, "You are your mother's daughter," or "You're just like Odessa." I laugh and say, "No, I'm not."

Recently it dawned on me that truly I am no longer my mother's daughter. I'm now a woman who had a mother. She influenced who I've become, and I count myself blessed to hold a deep and unquestioned respect for the kind of person Mom was. In hindsight, I can see that she never contorted herself to please others or cull favor. She stiffened her spine to get whatever resources she required to live the way she wanted. She rarely sought consensus or wasted time wondering. And I aspire to be more like her in those areas—want to lose any lingering tendencies to seek approval and beat myself up when I feel I've fallen short. I want her hard-nosed demeanor that shrugged off criticism or accepted blame for her transgressions without shrinking or fretting.

One Sunday at a Mother's Day program at her church, Mom was asked to share a message to young members of the congregation. I wondered briefly what in the world such an unsentimental woman who couldn't even fathom the concept of a "helicopter" mom would or could say to a room filled with tender-hearted parents. Mom stood. "It's hard to be a mother," she said. "A lot of times you don't know what to do or what you're doing. You can make a lot of mistakes. What I want to say to you is, don't be too hard on yourself. Everybody makes mistakes. But as you live, you learn. So, when you know better, do better. Do the best you can. That's what will get you through."

Tears came to my eyes because I'd made my share of parenting mistakes that weakened my spirit when they crossed my mind. Mom wasn't talking directly to me, but her message penetrated my heart and healed me a bit. Even now that my daughter is a grown woman, whenever I remember Mom's advice, it heals me a little bit more. It was a nugget of wisdom from her rarely revealed mother's heart.

Mom single parented me without ever complaining or uttering a syllable about hardship of any kind—even as I rebelled and struggled as a teen to find my own voice and path. She succumbed to some years of hard drinking, but never missed work or skipped a beat. As a landlord, she snaked drains, tarred the roof, kept the toolbox stocked, and maintained the property with the diligence and skills generally attributed to men. She worked hard without wearing herself out. Retired well and contented. Mom never found a companion to share her life with, but I don't believe she wanted one. She was always the strong one— the proud matriarch who welcomed and nurtured an extended family that cherished her. Who lived with such order that, after her death, I was able to locate any piece of documentation needed within minutes.

I learned so much from my mother's efficiency and business savvy, but her deepest desires and inner landscape will forever be mysteries to me. Until the end, she remained tight-lipped about many aspects of her relationship with my father. Offered no insights about heartbreak or joy, regrets or satisfactions. She left me to navigate affairs of the heart on my own. In time, I've recognized that there's no solace in chasing the tails of half-answered questions trying to tidy up loose ends. I've deemed such information irrelevant to my story. My sanity and well-being rest on truths that I've come to on my own. I'm grounded and more than prepared to get the most from my unfolding journey. Still, I rest easy knowing Mom's imprint reinforces me like double stitching in strategic places.

Figs

Gary Phillips

My father died and

I went down to pick his figs

Thinking to make a simple jam sweet

enough to absorb grief

Inside the humming tree – mid August

and hot enough to make snakes mad

I held a dancing

communion with yellow jackets,

red wasps, midge flies,

bumble bees, hornets, cow-killers;

working around the tree with

nimble, trembling fingers.

Did you know the great Bodhi tree was a fig?

That fig-milk dissolves warts?

That one can pray inside the circle of

A father's ancient anger and

not be stung?

Death Virgin

Camille Armantrout

When my mother's mother died, they laid her out in a cushioned casket and prettied her up. My eyes got as far as her hands before I chickened out. They had been painted orange and dusted with powder. I couldn't bear to see what they'd done to her face, so I turned away and stood next to my mother, inadvertently hiding my grandmother from all who had come to pay their respects. A column of people advanced towards us, and my mother gently moved me aside.

At 61, thirty years later, I was still a death virgin.

*****

Four years ago, my husband, Bob, and I were sitting on our back porch with some of our neighbors. We decided—not lightly—that we were strong enough to take on death. A new friend, Alisa, had learned that her husband, Chris, was dying of ALS and was seeking a safe port to ride out the storm and raise their three children. He had about a year to live, which would give our community plenty of time to figure out how to do home burials.

As they had done for us years before, Lyle and Tami gave Chris and Alisa a soft landing. And as predicted, that next spring Chris was edging closer to the grave with every breath.

In April, both Tami and Alisa were conspicuously absent from our monthly potluck. Tami arrived later having been at Alisa's. "How's it going over there?" someone asked. "Not good. I think we're close to the end." Our eyes widened. Death was coming, and we weren't ready. "Well, then it's time to start digging a grave," said Lyle and we had no doubt he would get on his orange Kubota the next day and break ground somewhere in the woods.

The next morning, my phone rang. Tami and Lyle's nineteen-year-old son, Zafer, had suddenly died—likely close to the time we were sharing dinner around our dining room table.

There are endless slices of this bittersweet pie. One hefty wedge is tart with shock. The news was unfathomable. "OD'd?" I said into the phone, "As in dead?" I sprinted down the trail, up the hill, and across the dam to Tami and Lyle's. The story came into focus. The sheriff had knocked on their door at midnight. A neighbor heard a howl rip through the woods. It was accidental, recreational.

Another piece is sweet with the power of community. A hundred hands reached out with food, lodging, transportation, music, and "anything at all"—an avalanche of goodwill that spoke to the beauty of our village. Dozens put their shoulders to a wheel that rolled forward until it stopped at a clay grave in the woods. Time sharpened to a point, and we all focused our energies on that point. I joined a burial committee, and with the help of a nine-tab spreadsheet, we juggled calls, texts, emails, and Facebook posts, matched offers to needs, and stayed on track.

The challenges of a do-it-yourself burial lent additional flavor to the pie. A few men marked out a meandering trail through sweetgum and loblollies, someone widened it with a Bobcat, and Lyle brought in his tractor and began digging the hole. Blinded by grief, he stepped down and his remaining son, Arlo, climbed up. The clay was so dense it broke the backhoe arm, and others finished the work using hand tools.

One person donated pine straw, and we spread the needles to cover the scars, making it look like any other dappled path through the woods. Another donated a set a granite obelisks to mark each end of the trail. Bob tied a strand of prayer flags from our garden between two trees and dubbed it the Farewell Trail. Chris arrived in his wheelchair to pick out his *own* gravesite.

We stood silent, admiring our work, breathing the scent of pine, listening to the knock of a woodpecker, and the soft "coo-OO-oo" of a mourning dove. I pictured myself at rest beneath the trees along the Farewell Trail and tasted peace, unexpected and nourishing. I haven't thought much about my burial, just as I don't think about the hotel bed when planning a vacation. Yet, no matter how excited I am to be somewhere new, I prefer to first check into the hotel, put down my bags, and glance at the bed. My adventures taste sweeter once I know where I'm going to sleep.

We held the memorial service in town and people poured in. After eulogies and music, Zafer took one last ride in his red Isuzu pup. Arlo took the wheel, his big brother behind him in a pine coffin with a wooden Z on the lid.

The burial was intimate, touching, heartbreaking, and real. No Astroturf. Just a pile of yellow clay and some borrowed shovels. Tami sat on the edge of the hole, throwing in handfuls until someone gently took her arm. Men, women, and children took turns until the job was finished, a mound of earth atop a wooden box.

*****

Six weeks later, I woke to Bob's honeyed voice saying, "Happy Birthday, dear." It was Saturday, June 4th, the day I would turn 62. I put some water on to boil and opened my card. It said, "Dream Big" with a little girl on a rocking horse casting a giant shadow of a woman astride a galloping horse, manes and tail flying. Inside he wrote, "Happy Birthday Love! Many, many, more. We're not done yet."

Sipping cocoa from a steaming mug, I picked up my phone and read a text. "Chris is dead," I said, "I'm going over." We held each other tight and I tried to imagine losing Bob. As I walked through the woods, I thought about this new slice of pie. I had been wondering whether an anticipated death was easier to swallow than an unexpected one and was about to find out.

I stepped into Alisa and Chris's bedroom, reaching out to touch Chris in passing. "Hey, Chris," I whispered. His leg felt thin and hard.

Alisa and her sister were sitting by the window, talking in hushed tones. I took a seat on the carpet. The kids were asleep outside the door, a puddle of blankets on the floor. Their three Boston bulls milled about. Chris lay silent, eyes closed, hands folded over his chest.

I had just received one of the most memorable birthday-presents of my life, the opportunity to touch a dead man.

Corpse dreams have always been a thing for me. Once I dreamed that I was peering into the face of a corpse, and realized I was looking into my own eyes. The flesh beside one eye was scarred and pinched. Horrified, I cried out to Bob, "Bunny! I'm dead..." and my voice was low and thick, like a slowed-down recording. In another dream, I found Bob inside a furnace, and I knew it was too late to save him. He was burned to ashes, and there was nothing I could do to bring him back. The horror of these dreams lingers.

Chris and I had a long chat the Wednesday before my birthday. He texted, and I talked. He was awash in anxiety, afraid of the unknown, and wished he knew what was going to happen to him after he died. I didn't have much to offer. This uncertainty is a piece of the pie that I had not considered. It's one thing to say you'll jump off a cliff, but standing up there, alone, with the wind ruffling your hair— that's an entirely different thing.

"What do you want to have happen?" I asked. I think we all have a different scenario in mind. For me, I just want my life to be over. I want to be done. The thought of spending eternity in heaven sounds arduous to me, but it's what my mother lives for. Chris said he didn't want to be alone. I said, "Well then, you won't be."

The next day he was no longer able to swallow. Alisa's family came in from out of state to join the stream of friends caressing Chris with music, flowers, and soothing words as he lay, heavily medicated. I kept myself busy outside, helping get the yard ready for a funeral. I wasn't prepared to see him like that. Maybe I'd bid him farewell Friday.

But Friday came and went, and I never got around to walking into the bedroom. The next time I saw Chris, he was laid out on the bed he built himself, atop the afghan his mother made for him, surrounded by dogs and roses. He looked a lot happier than he had on Wednesday.

I was happy, too. All my fears turned and marched off as soon as I walked into that room. If it turns out there is an afterlife, I'm going to look Chris up and thank him for helping me face my fears on my 62nd birthday.

*****

A few years went by without any burials. And then, in the spring of 2019, Barbara Lorie died at the age 93. I didn't know her well, but we swam in the same circles, occasionally crossing paths. I would turn a corner and feel the hum, a hive-like buzz that signaled Barbara's presence. She was charismatic, outspoken, and prone to profanity. Barbara's "Who are you?" had the disconcerting effect of pushing you off balance while putting you at ease. She was a teacher, a mother, an idealist, a civil rights advocate, and a fundamental force behind the creation of Blue Heron Farm Community.

On the morning of the funeral I noticed a string of pearls on top of my dresser. I had dug them out so I could give them to my oldest grandniece because she reminds me of myself in the way she takes responsibility for her younger siblings. Rather than take those pearls to my grave, I want to acknowledge her sacrifice. I will show her how to scrape her teeth lightly over one. "Does it feel slightly gritty?" I'll ask, "Like sandpaper?" That's how you know they are real.

I remember staying with my other grandmother, a woman we all called Nana and waking up one morning to find those pearls. Consciousness felt its way through the weave of the screens with the crow cries. Nana's bare feet plucked at the linoleum downstairs, moving toward the kitchen door where the dogs stood, fanning the air with their tails. I lay still, eyes closed. There was something else, an image, a niggling whisper.

Remembering how I had wrapped my final baby tooth in tissue, I slid my hand beneath the pillow. Usually, it was a coin, occasionally a dollar bill, and once a bar of halvah. I pulled out my prize, sat up and looked at a string of perfect pearls, exquisitely round and unmistakably grown up.

I hurried downstairs and found my Nana. She patted my bed hair, handed me a cup of coffee sweetened with honey and cream, and told me how an oyster takes an intruding bit of grit and surrounds it with soft smoothness to make a pearl. And that it can take years.

Pearls go great with little black dresses. I would wear them one last time.

Here was another wedge of pie: the ritual of honoring our ancestors. Each burial is an opportunity to savor memories, link them to the present, and take a look at where we fit in the march of time.

*****

Barbara wanted a raucous send-off, and that is what she got. She rested in her cardboard coffin atop a colorful wooden cart while we held hands in a big circle, and then, in her cart, she led the procession to the burial site. A brassy, Dixieland band came next, all drums and horns. They were followed by hundreds of mourner-celebrants, many carrying larger-than-life puppets, billowy silk banners, and giant orange and black butterflies. We all get to define the parameters of our send-off. Would we prefer a graham cracker crust, or one made of flour and butter?

We soon reached a large meadow with chairs facing a steep-sided red clay hole. A woman handed out programs, someone had put out drinking water, and a big pile of dirt waited on the far edge of the field. I chose a seat close to Lyle, a friend came and sat on my left, and Arlo joined us a little later.

The master of ceremonies kicked off a parade of tributes with some well-chosen words. One woman made us laugh with, "I was Barbara's favorite neighbor." Tami spoke of their long friendship and said that Barbara was looking forward to seeing Zafer. Many spoke about Barbara's enduring influence, about how her unabashed and forthright manner encouraged them to accept themselves. Several young people testified that her confidence—in herself, and in them—had had a profound impact on their lives and vowed to honor her memory by paying it forward.

When it was time to lower Barbara into her grave, I reached for Arlo's hand and undammed my tears. The group stepped forward, many pausing to drop peony petals or red clay into that straight-sided hole. I realized I was witnessing Barbara's legacy: the people she had touched and the community she had built.

Out came the shovels and three generations worked while others strummed guitars and sang. When the dirt was inches from the top, with another couple of loads to go, several people jumped in and began dancing on Barbara's grave. I wasn't sure how to think about this. My parents had made it very clear that stepping on someone's grave was a sign of disrespect, yet here was only joy. It made sense when I considered the alternative: a gas-powered tamper. We were over-writing the culture of death with new memes. No machines, no fake lawn, no orange hands.

All three funerals, Zafer's, Chris's, and Barbara's, showcase the power of community. Home burial is raw and real. There are no buffers. It is sweet with love, and tart with grief. Cemetery staff doesn't finish the dirty work; it's up to friends and families with shovels and hoes, in sandals and tennis shoes.

Losing Avery

Karen Howard

On a hot August day in the summer of 2002, at 22 weeks and three days pregnant, I lost my Avery Simone. Each of my previous pregnancies had been easy and without complications, so I thought nothing of going to this checkup alone. We were living in New Jersey at the time, and my then-husband stayed at home with our two- and three-year-old sons while the two older kids were at summer camp. I kind of enjoyed having a morning to myself and had stopped at Starbucks for a latte on the way in.

With this third pregnancy, my tummy had popped early and Avery was proving to be a kicker. Each time I ate or drank anything—long before the carbs could possibly have found their way into my bloodstream—her tiny legs would go from gentle butterflies delicately fluttering beneath my skin to giant moths hurling themselves at my belly button almost instantly. I couldn't decide whether she was excited by the approaching nutrient slush or reacting to the sounds of my state-of-the-art digestive system. Either way, I could tell that she was going to be feisty like her mother.

I'd secretly named her without consulting my husband—he'd gotten to name the boys. And I suppose it is one of the hallmarks of youth that we don't anticipate bad news. Instead, we hold fiercely to a comforting belief in the predictability, fairness, and perfection of the universe. That was the carefree spirit I was walking into my appointment that morning but not at all the young woman who walked out less than an hour later.

It has been 17 years and I can still picture with absolute clarity the puzzled look on my doctor's face as she searched for a heartbeat. I can remember focusing on the floral print of my maternity top as I tried to hold onto something that made sense. I remember my confusion and inability to understand the words that were coming from her lips. She was looking at me, but nothing she said could penetrate the fog. It was only when she put her arms around me that I began to process her meaning. I dissolved, alternating between angry and devastated.

How dare she not find a heartbeat!

Was she looking in the right place?

What does it mean? Try harder!

Try again. And again. And again.

Somehow, I made it home and must have told my husband because I can recall him holding me up as I fell to pieces in his arms. A few days later I went to Robert Wood Johnson Hospital in New Brunswick for the procedure to remove the tiny fetus from my uterus, and by the time I awoke, Avery was just a memory. I was wracked with sorrow and the overwhelming sense that I had let my precious baby down. I hadn't been there when she needed me most. How could I not have known she was dead? What kind of mother lets her baby die without even realizing it? What was I doing while she was fighting to live? The guilt was consuming.

I put myself to bed and over the next few weeks the love and comfort of my friends and family wrapped around me and ensured that kids were fed and entertained, dogs were walked, dishes washed, and kitty litter scooped. Some kind soul made sure that the tiny dresses and floral bedding I had purchased were returned to stores.

A few of the women in my circle shared stories of their own losses and reassured me that I would be fine and could try again soon. Some even pointed out how lucky I was to have gone through this before I became too attached to the baby. Some of them had suffered miscarriages later in pregnancy and seemed to have come through without any permanent scars. And in no time at all, it seemed to me that everyone else's lives returned to normal.

I cannot imagine the pain of losing a child whose face is familiar to me and whose smile lights up a room. I hope to never know the despair of watching a young life slip away from injury or disease. Those seem almost too hard to bear. But love and loss should not be a competition.

The death of a baby you longed for should count for something. The pain of one loss does not need to diminish the other.

I began to realize that the sympathy for my tears was a little less patient and the diplomatic steering of conversation away from my miscarriage more persistent. It was done gently, and perhaps even out of concern for me, but I wasn't done grieving and I couldn't just let her go. My tears retreated to the back of the master closet or to the shower behind locked bathroom doors so the kids wouldn't hear me. I moved into the guest room so my husband wouldn't be disturbed my crying at night.

There is an unspoken code of grief that dictates who gets to participate, who we are allowed to grieve and what that grief is supposed to look like. Although on an intellectual level I knew that miscarriage was a pain shared by far too many mother's before me, and despite having a loving family and a wonderful community of friends, I found that I would navigate the passages of grief alone because the world thinks a little differently about a baby that you've never actually held in your arms.

In many ways, I am lucky. I know that I have been abundantly blessed with health, love, a large unconventional family, and an incredible community of support. But at the same time, it bears saying that no one in any of my circles seemed to understand or expect the depth of the sadness that followed my miscarriage. Instead of holding and comforting me in that place, the focus very quickly turned toward helping me get over it and move on.

It took me some time to accept that every loss is individual and unique. Grief follows its own path. What may have only been an unnamed fetus to some, could be a child as loved and cherished as the ones I nursed and rocked to sleep—who I find myself falling in love with, over, and over again. Even today, so many years later, it is healing to tell the story of the precious girl I wouldn't get to know.

The weeks marched on and school opened, lunches had to be made, playdates scheduled, plants watered, and soccer games cheered. I was pulled back into the rhythm of family life and I found myself crying less frequently, allowing days to go by without calculating how far along my pregnancy would have been. We spent that Christmas in the Bahamas with my extended family, sailing, swimming and enjoying a little too much sun and fun.

After the miscarriage I would occasionally feel muscle spasms and I was still feeling some abdominal twinges when we returned home so I decided to return to my gynecologist for a checkup. I was pretty sure it was the result of a Herculean effort to help dislodge my brother's boat from a sand bar we got stuck on while vacationing, but I needed to be sure. After poking around on my belly for a few minutes and asking a thousand irrelevant questions, my doctor asked whether she could do an ultrasound because my abdomen felt distended.

We had skillfully avoided talking about the miscarriage at my request. Part of me still blamed her for not finding a heartbeat. Foolish—I know—but sometimes you just need something to hang your hurt on. As she probed around my abdomen with the ultrasound wand, I could see the expression on her face change. It's amazing the things you can find yourself willing to believe but for a fleeting moment I let myself think that she'd found the heartbeat, it had all been a terrible misunderstanding and

Avery was fine. But my rational brain knew that that could not be. Instead, I learned that I was two months pregnant with twins.

I was a little surprised—*okay*—completely stunned and a little confused. Her exact words were "Two heads, two strong heartbeats." My mind went everywhere. I will confess that for a moment, I thought she was referring to a two-headed baby. She quickly dispelled the notion. We were beyond happy!

Twin pregnancies are risky. After a loss, we should have considered that it was far too early to tell anyone—but we did it anyway. Ten weeks and five days. Friends, neighbors, and family joined in an extended carousel of support that remained consistent—even when I had to spend the final months on complete bed rest. Almost everyone was convinced that the twins were God's way of assuaging my loss. I was getting Avery back plus one.

The minister at our United Methodist Church felt that divine intervention was at the root of my twin pregnancy and that I was "blessed and highly favored." Complete strangers would proclaim that mother nature was giving me a gift. I wanted to believe it too, and I tried desperately for a while. I didn't want the twins to grow up feeling as though they were the consolation prize for the child I actually wanted. In my heart, they were always special unto themselves.

At 36 weeks and five days I gave birth to two sweet, perfect, beautiful baby boys. They completed our family and filled the house with a peaceful joy—the way only a baby-or-two can. They were loved tenderly, and doted on adoringly by their older siblings, and by two grandmothers who couldn't believe their incredible luck at no longer having to fight over who would get to hold the baby!

I was not expecting to become emotional again. But a few weeks after bringing the twins home, I found myself frequently in tears and thinking about Avery. It had been a year. Surely, I should be over the miscarriage by now and focusing instead on the precious boys in my arms. I could have passed it off as postpartum depression, but instead it seemed as though the birth had reawakened my despair over losing Avery.

One day while talking with my 86-year-old grandmother, I mentioned that I was still struggling and asked when I would get past it. "Never," she answered. She went on and shared the story of losing a baby at about 6 months pregnant in 1940. A girl she'd named Coralee. She was looking forward to seeing her again when she died. It had been 63 years and the thought of seeing Coralee comforted this wonderful woman who I'd always admired for her pluck, tenacity and joyful spirit.

Our relationship changed and deepened after that revelation. We shared stories of sorrow over losing our girls, but we also connected over finding the grace to go on and live fully and happily. She passed away when the twins were 8 and I imagine that she and Coralee are making up for lost time, even though I'm not convinced that there is an afterlife.

I know that I became a gentler mother when I finally gave myself permission to love my living children blindly and passionately and still miss Avery. I decided that I could be exceedingly grateful for the gift that each of my children represents and still wish she was amongst them.

And I do still miss her. I occasionally find myself wondering which of my boys she'd look more like and how being a girl would distinguish her from the rough, sweet, brave, young men her brothers have become. None of my kids are perfect. One is autistic, two suffer from depression, two have learning differences, and they *all* have questionable bathing schedules. But I love each one exactly as he is. I assume that Avery was imperfect too and that nature did what was best. But I sometimes wish that I could have let her know that I would have loved her anyway.

Being There

Jennifer Scanlon

I live in Maine, where the antelope don't roam.

In the simplest, most literal sense, I was *not there* for my mother, Marie—not there with her—when she passed away. That felt sad, and painful, and wrong. Although we lived only a mile apart in our small town of Brunswick and saw each other several times a week—when she lay dying in the nursing home at the age of ninety, I was three hundred miles away. Pacing up and down a terminal in LaGuardia Airport. Hoping to get back home to say goodbye.

In the end, I missed the chance not only to console my mother and help her make the transition from life to death but also to touch her, to hold her veiny, bony, strong and beautiful hands. To console myself by doing so. Her loss-of-life, and my loss, entwined in love and goodness and sorrow and death. Michael, my husband, sat with my mother on and off through her last night, and I knew she felt secure in his gentle care. But as a daughter I felt guilty, as a daughter almost inevitably might. I was on the tarmac when she passed, not with her.

Since my mother's passing, I have had more than sufficient time to reflect instead, or at least as well, on how I *was there* for her, how I was present as the pall of dementia gradually crept in to define her daily existence and force her toward death. What does it mean to be there for someone as they die of a gradual but commanding disease like dementia? What does it mean to help another person through the dissolution and desolation of an illness we still know so little about?

I was her companion, caregiver, and advocate. I was there to share in the flavors she and I enjoyed in our everyday lives: crumbs from a piece of coffee cake, cups of black tea with milk, saltine crackers in plastic packets, bites of a crab cake, vanilla ice cream cups with paper lids that pull off at the tabs.

I was there to convince nursing home staff that giving my mother less food rather than more would encourage her to eat. I was there to take her out, even in the most inclement Maine weather, so she could see my family, or feast her eyes on strangers on sidewalks, and feel a distance, however brief, from the fluorescent lights and lukewarm coffee of the place she could never reckon as home. I offered her diner pancakes, supermarket outings, news of children and grandchildren and great grandchildren, drives to the coast, foot massages, tenderness and laughter, and, importantly, memories.

Memories. Shared memories. We had so many, and those we chose to recall were, at first, comfort-giving, laughter-inducing, occasionally sentimental. We enjoyed each other's company and our shared pasts, and memories helped us find our way, incrementally, through a profound transformation from independence to dependency.

Shared memories of my mother's presence at the center of our household had a special resonance for each of us during that stage of her life and care, and we found ourselves laughing most over things domestic: a mouse that had once lived in our oven, the unwieldy books of wallpaper samples my mother would borrow and haul home from the wallpaper store, the way she would touch the couch when she returned from work to determine if the dog had spent the day sleeping on it, the unspoken rule about Mom's "Milky Way drawer" in the kitchen. These reminiscences felt mutual, simple, and lovely; they provided a languorous means of spending time together as the early stages of dementia brought not so much memory loss or confusion as tiredness and frailty.

As the disease took greater hold, my mother's memories morphed. We entered a disquieting phase in which even the simplest memories began to feel more murky, fluid, and contestable. It was hard, but it was also here, in the vexed space of dementia-challenged memory, that I began to understand that being there for my mother meant being with dementia—embracing my mother meant embracing dementia, finding ways to laugh and feel joy through the disease and its progression, not in spite of it. I had to learn to enjoy something that was frightening and foreboding.

Memory loss, like memory itself, is a bit mercurial. It was one thing when my mother and I remembered the same things, but differently: she most often remembered how well we got along, and how our frames of reference overlapped, while I too often remembered our spats and our differences. It was another thing, though, when the disease progressed. Her memories began to shapeshift, and her ability to locate them at will diminished. Our source of shared pleasure—memory—became the space where dementia most visibly exercised its cruel dominion, threatening our connection.

How would we, individually and together, face and handle the protracted demise of something so fundamental to human existence and relationships as memory? And what was to be my role in relating to my mother's increasingly erratic, surprising, unreliable, and missing memories? How could I help her live with dementia's privations?

At first—unexpectedly and to my delight—the shifts in my mothers' ability to recollect encouraged in me my own set of acute memories. I pulled things up from the recesses, recalling for brief but intense periods various sets of remembrances.

I remember weeks of recalling images, sounds, and smells from our many family trips to the ocean: long days spent witnessing the tides turn and then turn again, that shortness of breath that comes from swallowing too much salt water, my mother's homemade lemonade, the hand-painted lamps we won on the boardwalk arcade, the tightness of sunburned limbs pressed against other sunburned limbs on car rides home, losing out in quarrels over which of the six kids got into the shower first, or second, or third. It made sense: my parents both loved the ocean, I learned to love it from them, and sitting quietly with my mother furnished the time and space for recall. I spent so much time thinking about the ocean that I inevitably began to craft metaphors about my mother's situation, focusing on dementia's small currents, crushing waves, dislocating undertows. Perhaps I was trying to convince myself that my mother's deteriorating condition was natural, as inevitable as the tide. I wish I could say I succeeded, but that too was gradual.

Instead, and for too long, I viewed dementia as something to fight, particularly in the arena of memory loss or dislocation. I engaged passionately—if futilely—in resistance, trying to retain, regain, or recreate "normal" life with and for my mother, reminding her of the memories I hoped she could hold on to, as though reminders could somehow mitigate the encroachments of disease, and as though that was caregiving.

"Yes, you remember going to this restaurant, Mom," I would prompt, hoping to spark a memory I thought she needed to access.

"No, Mom, you didn't know Marilyn when you lived in the Bronx," I would say, trying to correct a recollection that had come out in twisted strands, unrecognizable to those who had been there.

I considered it my duty, for a time, to help my mother keep verifiable memories at the center and push questionable memories to the periphery. A noble cause, replete with scorekeeping: occasionally rewarding, ultimately exhausting.

I relished her victories and still enjoy telling our few triumphant tales. One day, when my mother was experiencing complications with her heart, two EMTs came to take her to the hospital. To verify she was their patient, one of them asked her the date, which she could not provide. *Who could?* I ask, *living day after day in the indeterminate space and time of a nursing home.* He then asked her who was the President, and she told him it was George Bush. Senior or junior, the man wanted to know. "George W.," she informed him, not testily but firmly. "He's not a junior." One for our side.

Another day, we waited in my mother's room for a visit from an insurance company nurse whose task it was to determine if my mother really belonged in assisted living—or if she could instead fend for herself. I was cringing at my mother's Catholic-school-bred determination to get a perfect score on the test. She failed the intake interview, demonstrating that she needed the level of care of assisted living; remarkably, she also nearly passed it. Another one for our side, sort of.

Over time, I realized the fight was futile. But more than that, I realized that it had become my fight. My mother was entering a new stage of life, one that included clear moves toward even more significant memory loss, toward death. To embrace my mother, and our days together, I had to embrace the disease and its strange manifestations: snippets of clarity, moments of partial recall, seeming fabrications, recollections just beyond our collective grasp. I had to let go of the empirical and find joy in the muddy middle. I'm so glad I did, so glad I embraced a new way, cultivating the relationship through dementia, to *be there* for my mother.

When my mother saw animals roaming around in the field outside of her bedroom window, did it matter that I didn't see them, as long as their presence didn't frighten her? We took pleasure in trying to name them. *Antelope,* she decided. *Certainly not, in Maine.* But we went with it. When we discovered that antelope rhymes with cantaloupe, we had some good laughs. Surrendering to antelope was so much less stressful than promoting rabbits.

Did it matter that I had never before heard of the boyfriend she told me her doctor reminded her of? Was he real, one of the many people from a long ago past who began to inhabit her consciousness during the disease's progression, or was he manufactured of the whole cloth of dementia? I never found out, but in the ensuing conversations, which I learned to engage in joyously, I learned a thing or two about the young Marie, the single career woman I had not after all had the pleasure of knowing.

When I let go of my empirical bent, and perhaps in part because I let go of it, my mother also took me on a few months' journey to her mother, Rose. She talked regularly about making arrangements for her mother to visit, picked out flowers for her mother at the farmer's market, instructed me about where they would sit and visit when Rose arrived. I knew that my grandmother had had a hard life, but I heard more about my grandmother through the fog of dementia than I had heard in years of my mother's lucid but reticent recollections of times past and in some ways, perhaps, better forgotten. I learned how close my mother had been to her mother, and I felt a new closeness to mine.

I was not able to say goodbye to my mother in person, but perhaps a gift of dementia was that she and I practiced goodbye over time and in incremental ways, each marked, to be sure, by loss: a depletion of mobility, a distortion of memory, a movement to dependency. Dementia took away so much—ultimately, it took my mother's life—but to be *with* my mother on that journey, I had to accept the disease and its strange and mysterious meanderings, particularly those that challenged my notions of what it means to recollect. I had to accept new definitions of memory, of truth, of my mother. And really, are my own memories— even of that time—reliable? Or are they too fickle, distorted by love, desire, anger, grief?

I do know this for certain: I miss my mother, but as I remember it, we had some good laughs in those days, sipping our tea while the antelope roamed.

The Gifts of Death

Leif Robert Diamant

When I was fourteen, my dad packed a suitcase in the morning—as if he were going somewhere.

"Are you going to work?"

He replied, "My father died yesterday from a heart attack, and I'm flying to New York for the service." I hadn't known that Grandpa Harry had been ill.

And then this rare and strange phenomenon happened—my dad had tears welling in his eyes. He wiped his eyes quickly and left for the airport.

This was the first encounter with death in my family during the first fourteen years of my life.

Death was a mysterious, ambiguous, and uncomfortable topic—not to be discussed in the family that I grew up in. The loss that I struggled with from having been abused and neglected as a young child was even more taboo. As uncomfortable as death was, being separated from my birth mother or siblings at the age of seven was even worse.

My father Louie and stepmother Ann wanted our family to fit into the American Dream of normality and success. My experiences and all the unhealed trauma they caused were disturbing to them and to me. I went along with the pretense and hid my inner life with a young child's lack of awareness.

Around my eighteenth birthday, I wanted to know about my mother Sonia. I wanted to see her. I was angry and weary from this secret life of denying my mother, pretending Ann wasn't my stepmother. I was confused about what was going on in me, as though there were some deep disturbance in my psyche.

With great trepidation, I mustered the courage to ask my father.

"Do you know where Sonia is? I want to see her."

"Your grandmother Helene called yesterday. Sonia just died."

I was flabbergasted and felt something akin to being sucker punched.

I angrily spewed out, "Weren't you even going to tell me?"

He awkwardly muttered something along these lines, "Of course, I was…"

I burst into tears and went outside.

Later that day, he told me that she had died from a heroin overdose. I do not remember any further discussion, but he did invite me to go to New York City with him on a business trip and we would see my grandmother.

In Manhattan, we went to her apartment on Riverside Drive by the Hudson River. When we entered, I was immediately aware how dark her home was. The mirrors were draped with black shawls. And she was crying and burning a candle on a plate with a photo of my mother on it.

Her grief was so heavy to me. I hadn't thought that she would be in mourning. I didn't even have the concept of mourning in my awareness. I had no previous exposure to Sitting Shiva, which is the Jewish mourning ritual for grieving and healing. I had been brought up without religion and my parents—somewhat proudly—called themselves atheists.

My grandmother wept and talked about her loss. My dad probably said something, but I don't remember what. I was speechless. Unemotional. And I felt a storm inside of me, filling me with discomfort. No tears or anger.

My mother died at age 39.

*****

That storm has been ravaging and healing me throughout the rest of my life. In my early childhood, I shut down and it took a lot of years to open back up. To learn to cry. To be able to feel rage. To be vulnerable. I learned that my failures and fears were gifts. Not parts of me that must be buried again and again.

This was the beginning of my ongoing journey to be fully human. To live with my true self without hiding from it.

Since then, as a licensed psychotherapist and ordained minister, I have assisted people with terminal illnesses and dying. And over the years, I've also had some not-very-close friends and relatives die. But my first truly intimate experience with death came in 1995, nearly thirty years after the death of my mother Sonia.

My stepmother Ann—who functioned as my only mother after my seventh birthday as an outcome of two custody trials—was diagnosed with breast cancer that had gone into remission. She didn't say that it might be recurring, and I hadn't been wondering. In the Spring of 1995, I had a dream:

I'm with Ann, my mom, and her head looks skeletal. She asks me to help her move a couch but has no physical strength. I ask her what's wrong. She doesn't say. I ask if she's dying. She still doesn't respond. I start crying. She tells me to stop crying. I tell her, choking back tears and anger. "Don't tell me not to cry. I'll cry if I want."

I called her and asked, "Has your breast cancer returned?"

She replied, "I've recently seen my oncologist and he said that I'm okay."

I left my farm in Silk Hope and drove to Charlotte, feeling a high level of urgency and alarm. When I got to Ann's house, I thought that she didn't look well.

I asked her to make an appointment with the oncologist so I could attend. The next day we met in the non-medical part of his office. He downplayed the return of symptoms. When I pushed harder, he very reluctantly revealed that he suspected the cancer had metastasized. He suggested she start chemotherapy.

The first round of chemotherapy sickened and weakened her noticeably. She never felt well after that and decided not to do more treatment. I supported her decision since the chemotherapy seemed to be an intolerable poison to her. And the cancer was now spreading aggressively.

I was going through custody struggles for my three daughters and was feeling more lost than I had felt in a long time. I made the decision to be with my mom during her passage through sickness into death.

As I drove back to Charlotte, I prayed to the Universe to help me be of service to her. I wanted to let go of my many unresolved issues around my stepmother.

Ann was controlling, critical, and cold with me; all the while, she treated her birth daughter with much praise, warmth, and specialness. She had often slapped me across the face when I was bratty, challenging, or 'talking back.' Those slaps were far more humiliating than painful, and I had hated her for them throughout my childhood.

When I was fifteen years old, I put an end to it by grabbing each of her hands as she attempted to hit me and holding them. I shouted firmly "Never slap me again!" The next and last time she went to slap me, I blocked her slap and started laughing. This transition was never discussed.

When I entered into her death care, I wanted to give my mom dying comfort, care, and love. As Ann grew sicker, a very strange thing happened. I started to feel this love for her. Although she had no interest in discussing dying or death, she was more open and seemed freer than I had ever experienced. And instead of me bringing up anything from the past to resolve, she expressed her regret for many things that she had either done *to* me or had failed to do *for* me.

I accepted her apologies with gratitude, and I had some for her that she certainly deserved to hear. I felt a deep joy and increasing love for her, literally feeling ecstatic at times being with her. She did more than I could have imagined. She dealt with the emotional aspects of our earlier times together in a way that was comforting and healing for me, and I gave her back love and forgiveness.

*****

My dad, Louie, died last November in Charlotte. He was just past 97. After a rare visit to the hospital in his early nineties, he demonstrated his vigor by doing one hundred push-ups in front of the hospital medical team in hopes of being discharged. And it worked.

At 95, my father slipped on his tile bathroom floor while peeing and broke his hip. This was by far the worst physical injury of his life. Not only did he have to go back to the hospital, he also went to a residential rehabilitation clinic for a few months.

Between my mother's death and Louie's accident, I deepened my study of dying and death. I went to some classes, read some books, helped others with their dying process. I officiated a few funerals and memorial services, gave some presentations and taught classes. My own health issues and a near death experience were motivating me to learn from death by helping others.

When I visited my dad in rehab, I brought a copy of Advanced Directives so he could make choices about the care he wanted and *didn't* want. He was extremely uncomfortable with the document and said he'd deal with it later—which he never did.

He was in rehab for several months and went home with a healed hip. He lived in his home with his partner Teri who was forty years younger.

His first day home, while watching television, he dropped the remote control. Bending to pick it up, the chair and he fell over—toppling an even heavier chair onto his leg. His femur broke. He returned to the hospital and residential rehab once more.

My dad became very depressed, somewhat confused, and unable to walk. He had impressed people with his ability to do the physical therapy exercises when his hip was broken. But the broken femur was demoralizing and clearly, he was in decline.

When he returned home six months later, I brought the Advanced Directives again.

He didn't want to see them at all. He told me he didn't want to talk or think about "it."

During a subsequent visit, he revealed, "I'm awake through the night. Afraid and worrying."

"What are you afraid of Dad?"

"Not being here?"

I asked him, "How is being here now?"

"Kind of depressing," he muttered.

"It probably would be okay not to be here…" I said.

That was the end of that conversation.

I did think of things to say to help him in this process, though I never said many of them. Mostly I'd hang out with him, holding his hand, chatting until he got tired. I'd set up time for just him and I to talk alone in case he wanted to share something from his inner life. Or in case I had something to offer that might comfort or assist him in truly comprehending the inevitable process that was happening to his body.

One time, I sloppily quoted Ram Dass.

"Dying is safe Dad. Everybody does it successfully."

He awkwardly chuckled.

I encouraged him to look back at his life, remembering things he felt good about and people he loved who also loved him. He said that he felt guilty about so many things. I encouraged him to imagine healing those relationships and having conversations with those people that made things right again.

In one of our last conversations, my dad said "I don't know how I got in this situation. If only I hadn't fallen, I would not be in this mess."

I replied "I just read that the oldest person in the world died. She was 114 years old. So, no matter what, your time would be up in less than twenty years."

I looked over at him to see how he was processing this wise jewel.

His mouth was open, and he was asleep.

A few weeks earlier, much to his objections, hospice had set a bed up in his living room.

My dad got on that bed. And as he laid down, he died—probably just like he wanted to die.

Without awareness. As if he was taking a nap.

A Glimpse into a Legacy

Dori DeJong

It was an unseasonably warm day in mid-April 2016 when we walked along the gravel road. My husband was dressed in a long sleeve light blue shirt and tie, dress pants, dress shoes, and sunglasses. He sweated profusely and appeared exhausted from the long walk in the heat. While we were attending the funeral of a buttoned-down family, my husband was still very much a buttoned-up man.

As far as he was concerned, we were attending a funeral. Funerals are formal occasions that demand a certain dignity and respect from attendees. This was how he showed respect—by wearing his respectful clothes.

My husband, two daughters, and I were attending a large community Celebration of Life for a sweet young man who'd had his entire life ahead of him. Residents, friends, and family alike were crowded onto the grounds. Many were sitting under a large tent in folding chairs, others out in the sweltering heat holding fans. Some were wearing festive hats and interesting shoes, a request from the boy's father because the boy had liked hats and shoes.

Our youngest daughter was a participant in this ceremony. She was the young man's longtime childhood girlfriend. She was so much a part of the family that they still regarded her as his girlfriend, even though the two had not been dating since their senior year of high school. She was in her Sophomore year in college in North Carolina, and he was in his Sophomore year out in Colorado.

They still loved each other. They talked often. Our daughter had talked to him the day before he died.

As we approached the seating area before the ceremony, we looked for our youngest daughter who was huddled with the family and other participants. We found the large tent seating area, which was full. When one of our daughter's friends saw my husband and how much he was sweating, she gave up her seat for him so he could sit out of the hot sun.

You see, my husband was a chemo patient. My husband was dying from terminal Colon Cancer.

I was not able to sit with him, so I found another seat. The ceremony began with music and kind words, a community wrapping its proverbial arms around a grief-stricken family. My husband sat stoic in his seat, sweating, exhausted, with his Oakleys over his blue eyes.

Individual speakers—some friends, some family— told stories about this young man and his short, vibrant, and impactful life.

Over the years, I've attended other events such as this, and they are usually both sad *and* happy affairs. However, this one was just sad. There was nothing about the abrupt ending of a nineteen-year old's life that could possibly be happy. There was no way to sugarcoat that simple reality with funny, whimsical stories or laugh-worthy memories. Of course, people tried. What else can you do?

The time came for our desperately bereaved daughter to give her part of his Eulogy. She walked up to the stage and stood in front of the microphone. She wore a short skirt and held the printout of her own prepared speech. She read it to the crowd, sharing many of the details and sweetness that was the totality of a seven-year period of her own short life spent with this young man. The relationship, really a centerpiece of those years. Her dying father sat in the crowd, head tilted down, listening to a glimpse of his own future Eulogy.

After the scripted portion of the ceremony concluded, family members were receiving hugs and condolences from attendees. The young man's father stood off to the side. My husband and I walked up to him. I hugged him and then he shook my husband's hand. And as our daughter walked up to us, my husband grabbed her and held her and cried, sobbing loudly into her neck. Not for this boy who just died. Not for his grieving father.

But for her.

He heard that overwhelming pain she was carrying in her latest stage of acute and profound loss. He knew that she was holding not only the burden of this young man's untimely death but the burden of his impending, slow and horrifying end. She was only nineteen years old—just a baby, really—and he knew that she would have to go through this again. And soon. And that she would be sharing stories and memories and intimate details of a daughter's heart about her daddy.

And he wouldn't be there to hold her or comfort her or support her for any of it. He would be powder in a tin can with flowers on-top, next to an American flag.

*****

Just under six months after that horrible day, we attended another Celebration of Life event in honor of my husband and the life he led: a life of honor and integrity and love. My father-in-law gave a eulogy. My husband's best friend gave a eulogy. Our eldest daughter gave a eulogy. Our youngest daughter gave a eulogy. And I gave a eulogy.

The space was standing room only. A horde of people attended, several from out of state—work colleagues, company executives, college classmates, local friends and neighbors. Some were friends of our daughters or people who never knew my husband but who wanted to be supportive. The American flag out front was lowered to half-mast for him.

While my husband was not that nineteen-year old—his life, too, was inexplicably cut short. A year before his death, he experienced a strange and unrelenting back pain. That pain eventually turned into colon surgery, which then turned into Stage Four Colon Cancer—a diagnosis he received the day before his forty-seventh birthday.

As time continued to churn on around him, his life – as he knew it – was over.

Mine was too, but in a different way. I became the person who had to watch an otherwise healthy, active, hard-working man not only waste away without any chance to live, but also watch him grapple with the torment of knowing it was happening—seeing the terrified look in his family's face.

*****

At some point, most of us will think about our own mortality and our own funeral. Who would come? Who wouldn't? What would be said about our lives and our memory? My husband was no different.

When he first learned that he was going to die, we attempted to talk about what I needed to do with him after he was gone. His first response was that he did not want me to have a service because "no one would come and that would be embarrassing."

Even in the depths of his pain, he believed that no one would care enough about him to attend a ceremony in honor of his life.

But he was wrong. And like a typical wife, I was happy to tell him so in my Eulogy as I looked out into a crowded room of all the people who cared.

There are few silver linings in the endless dark clouds of watching the man you love die.

My husband started a journal. He was not what you would call a "journal guy," so it was very uncharacteristic of his personality. He wanted to document his own life and his challenges with coming to terms with the end of it. I believe this very personal and intimate journal project was prompted by the glimpse he received of his own funeral that day when they lowered a sweet boy into a deep hole within the Carolina red clay.

Because he ran out of time and died much quicker than we ever imagined, my husband did not have the opportunity to write letters to his girls, his parents, his sisters, his friends, or even to me. But the journal became a sort of letter for us all—of what he would have written to us. A piece of his Legacy.

That journal was his witness to the end of his own life, his expressions of fears and regrets, what he would miss out on, and how profoundly sad he was to be leaving us at such a key time in his life. The journal addressed how his sadness was compounded by how much pain we would all have to contend with while left to figure out how to live our lives without him here.

*****

Because of the tragic death of that young man, my husband had a preview of his own funeral by watching our strong, deeply talented and resilient daughter give words of love, hope, and encouragement. It made him see firsthand just how much his death would impact not only her but the rest of us who loved him.

But his death is only one piece of the impact. Death is only the part where it's unimaginably sad. The cruel joke here is that we think death is the end of a life. And yes, in some ways it is.

But then there is a new life left behind. And that is Legacy.

My husband got a glimpse into his Legacy. He was young enough for his end to be a downright tragedy, but old enough to have left a lasting and rich Legacy behind. He touched so many lives while alive, and he had no idea just how many. And do any of us ever really know? Of course not.

Everything we do during the course of our lives becomes a part of our Legacy. That's why our actions and deeds are so very important. All the time. The musical Hamilton sings, "Legacy. What is a legacy? It's planting seeds in a garden you never get to see."

What kind of seeds did my husband plant that he never got to see?

They are endless.

So much has happened in the few short years he has been away.

Our eldest daughter is out on her own, working for a major hospital, back in nursing school full time, and engaged to be married. She is doing what he said he knew she would do within his journal:

She wants to be a nurse and is working quite hard to achieve that goal. She has had a few setbacks along the way, but each time she has gotten back on track. I'm certain that she will eventually reach her goal – even if she has a few more bumps in the road along the way. It's not likely that I'll be around to see her complete this journey, but I know she'll make it. Whatever credit I am due for the type of person that Abby has grown into is clearly one of the most significant and proudest achievements of my life. She has grown into a wonderful young woman who is committed to her principles and does her own thing no matter how outside the norm she is. I'm incredibly proud of her and want nothing more than to see her achieve her goals and build a good life for herself. I just wish I could be around to continue helping her in whatever way I can.

After graduating from college, our youngest daughter is serving in Africa with the United States Peace Corps, now in her second year. This was never a goal in her life before both tragedies became a centerpiece of her story. My husband was particularly worried about her losing him and was scared for her, as he lamented his journal about his impending death:

It breaks my heart that she's going to have to go through some of the most critical years of her life without a father. I always thought I would have more of an influence on both girls as they make the transition into adulthood. I figured I would help them with all the practical things of adult life and make sure they knew how to take care of themselves. Ally will probably suffer more with the consequences of me not being around.... I just hope that the enormous gap that will form after I'm gone can be filled somehow by someone.... I don't know how to help her through this even if I did have the emotional strength to do it. Hopefully she'll find a way to get though it and move ahead with her life. I'm sure she will, but it might get a bit rough for her.

He had no earthly idea the non-traditional path she would blaze for herself to fill that enormous gap, learn to take care of herself, make the transition into adulthood and move ahead with her life. And yes, it has been *a bit rough*.

I know that he would be so tremendously proud of the seeds he planted and what they have grown into since he's been gone. He would be so, so proud of the Legacy he left behind within these strong, independent, resilient, thoughtful, and hardworking young women. These girls are both a walking, living, breathing embodiment of every great thing he was as a man.

The Difficulty and the Gift I Carry Toward Death

Gary Phillips

(I come to this writing task like a man who faces a machinery he might lose a finger to, like a kosher butcher who makes her prayers to God with fear and trembling, afraid they might be answered.)

Last night I went to bed bruised and blue, as I have for several days. I perceive now that I spoke sharply to my lover in a way that made her ambivalent about coming to bed with me, much less being tender with me, something I wanted so deeply I was afraid to ask for it.

I knew that my testiness and agitation, my ragged lack of patience, was connected somehow with an angry tumultuous conversation I had with my best friend yesterday, but I could not untangle my feelings from my reactions. They each withdrew from me a bit, friend and wife, wounded by my raging animus.

So, I went to bed alone. At the door of sleep, I floated an inchoate question: What is my path forward or backward, where are the markers, what restless spirit animates and endangers me?

The image which built itself piece by piece from that moment until it woke me at 3AM was whole and stark and piercing: my friend Ruffin's body broken on the rocks under his tall house and not found for hours, pelted at by rain and wind.

My dream body caught its breath and understood. Waking, I released the tears which had threatened to drown me whole.

So, here it is. I am a vulnerable man in my fifties, surrounded and permeated by loss (personal-ecological-political), not so much afraid of my own death as I am of my frailty, of the inevitable demise of the people I love, and of who I will be without them.

In this case, I wanted my beloveds to be present so deeply as a hedge against brother death that I tested them (my "testiness") with a sharper regard to see if they bled, to assure myself that they were not phantoms, that I would find them warm and connected to me in the sympathetic restless light of morning.

This is not unfamiliar to me. I know I can react this way to precipitous events, where I literally feel myself out over a chasm of change, of possibility, of a deep and necessary regret. This has been a year of so many funerals.

I *want* to solidify in the deepest possible way what is real in my life, but I don't have the right to fearfully rattle the cages of my relationships and frighten the people I love. I step back consciously from that precipice, set about repairing the bridge, commit to a generous daily life of support and engagement.

To the most important people in my life: this does not take you off the hook of my hard love. I have apologies to extract as well as give, conflicts to resolve in the context of relationship-building. I don't always like the way you do things or how you treat me, and I want us to talk with candor about our feelings. I promise to listen, and to be tender.

One of the legacies of death's corona is an urgency to talk about difficult issues, an impatience with the surface of things, a courage to dive into dark waters. I'm choosing to accept that gift. Life is short. Engage with me.

Women's Work

Hannah Eck

Mom hasn't slept for days. I can see it in the distance of her eyes, hear it in the flatness of her voice. Her exhaustion runs bone deep. I could sense it on the phone, long before I walked through the door. Inside the little house, the air is thick with dying smells. Stale sweat. Acrid breath. The sharp tang of urine. The sickly sweet of morphine. And something else that I can't quite name.

Grandma is lying in a bed in the corner, the log walls framing her like a photograph. The window high above the room is awash with sun, lighting up the little sparkly bits of dust floating in the air. Around her head, white curls tumble to a perfect halo. Her honey warm skin is as translucent as beeswax, as though you could see right into the veins below. Her deep blue eyes are sunken. Her lips cracked and parted just so.

She's gone already, I think to myself.

I take timid steps from the kitchen to the living room, edging slowly towards her bed. The sun is in my eyes and I can feel the tears brimming. I lay my hand on hers. "Grandma." It comes out as a whisper. She takes a sharp breath, whips her head towards me, and shoots up out of bed, her eyes wild as a boar. "KILL IT! KILL IT!" she screams. "MOOOOTHER! Kill that CAT!"

*****

Grandma decided to die one morning in February. She had made up her mind. It was her time, and no one dared to argue with her. After a decade of dementia, it was a miracle that she made this decision at all. Decisions are few and far between when your mind starts to go. And my grandma had been living between worlds for quite some time.

Grandma stopped eating and drinking. Mom made calls. I drove 276 miles—winding my way up through the clouds to the heart of the Appalachian Mountains that had once been my home.

In the early 90's, my grandparents left their conventional lives and took to the hills. They spent every dollar they had on a fourteen-acre lot in the middle of nowhere on the most beautiful mountain God has ever known. No electricity. Ridgeline to ridgeline. Didn't own a thing. Didn't know a soul. Nothing for miles but hairpin curves and mountain laurel. A bubbling spring fed their reservoir while the land nourished their souls. The only structure standing was a hand-hewn, one-room schoolhouse that dated back to the Confederacy. With a Willys Jeep, a chainsaw, and a winch—they built a home.

*****

By the time I arrived, hospice had brought a hospital bed. Mom worked some magic on a corner in the living-room, turning it into a cozy little sleeping place. Grandma was dying exactly how she had imagined—in the log cabin her husband had built by hand all those years ago.

*****

Mom has gone to bed and I am alone with Grandma as she floats in and out of consciousness.

She wakes and asks me when we're supposed to be leaving. Can I find her shoes, *please?*

She wakes and asks if I'm depressed and recommends some meditation cassette tapes.

She wakes and points and screams for me to kill that cat again. *Mother, kill it. Kill it now!*

She wakes and looks for the bite of peanut butter she's dropped onto the couch cushion.

She wakes and asks why I am doing this to her. *Noooo! Why, would you do this to me?*

She wakes and orders a glass of red wine, though she gave that up decades ago.

Grandma is submerged in the flow of a great river, travelling within. Calmness takes her under. Her breathing slows until it's almost imperceptible. Violently, she comes back to the surface. Gasping for air in a jolt of incandescent lucidity—she emerges into a different moment in her wild and wondrous life.

Her neural pathways must be firing off at random. Or maybe there are ghosts visiting and only she can see them between worlds. For fourteen hours, Grandma and I relive her life together—almost always circling back to me as her mother.

My great grandmother had a voice smooth as Maker's Mark. I'm the spitting image of her—from the top of my head to the tips of my toes. We don't often talk about my great grandfather. The only thing I know about him is that he had hurt his children in a very deep and scarring way and that my mama wouldn't ever let me sit on his lap as a young child.

*****

A beaded buckskin bag holding a mason jar of my grandfather's ashes.

An old clay horse that's been on my mom's shelf for decades.

A ceramic tile that Uncle Todd had painted her for Mother's Day.

A brass bell—she loved those. Seashells and rose quartz—she loved those too.

A braid of sweetgrass from Brooke Medicine Eagle—one of Grandma's teachers.

A little wicker baobab tree because she always wanted to go on safari in Africa.

A bit of fluorite for a smooth transition. A candle to be extinguished when she crosses the river.

A faded high school photo of her sister, Aunt Gin. They had lost touch.

A feather that I had harvested from a barred owl dead on the side of the road the month prior.

Grandma had once saved an injured owl from the road in the dead of night. She wrapped it in a towel she found in the backseat of her car and drove it home. It sat still, swaddled in her lap for all those miles. Grandma nursed it back to health in the barn, and it continued to roost in our woods for what seemed like years.

One by one, Mom and I place these items on a small table at her bedside: a dying time altar for a wild and wondrous life well-lived.

*****

I have always heard that a body can only go a week without food and three days without water before dying. Grandma is on day ten.

A slight madness has taken our household. Mom has stopped sleeping again and I've started hitting the bottle of Maker's around the clock. I leave my almost empty glass on the altar directly atop Aunt Gin's high school photograph, encapsulating her in a yellow, watery moon.

In the first few days, we had a steady stream of visitors to give us reprieve from the slow hell of watching Grandma die. Neighbors. Coworkers. Clients. Friends. Just a single hour away from bedside was all we needed to get through the next twenty-three. We even had one of our closest family friends spend two days nursing Grandma. But it's now day ten.

Grandma's moments of lucidity are sparse but more violent now, and it has become painfully evident that she's reliving her sexual trauma again and again. She still believes that I'm her mother and I feel helpless, watching her struggle against memories of her father's touch. I sit at the top of the bed, stroking her fine white hair, and singing her gospel songs. When she struggles, I hold her hands tightly so that she can't pull out her catheter. She wriggles and clenches her knees closed. A piece of me is dying inside, right there with her.

The egg that each of us came from developed in our mother's ovaries when she was a baby—at four months gestation—developing in her own mama's belly. This means that our original cell, our very potential, is intrinsically linked to our Grandmother's being. I can only imagine what stories we hold deep in our genes.

The Iroquois have a Great Law that one must make decisions for seven generations ahead of one's own self— approximately 140 years. Coincidentally, it also takes seven generations for an adaptation to occur in any organism. You can see this in factory chickens, whose generations are much shorter than our own. A seventh-generation caged chicken will never walk, even when set free in one of God's greenest pastures. The trauma Grandma is working through will reverberate through four more generations after me, down to my great-great-great grandchildren.

*****

We were no strangers to death, Mom and I. Our little family had put Grandpa Ray to rest just nine months earlier. With him, we followed our culture's standard dying formula. Hospital to hospice. Mortuary to grave. Ashes to ashes. Dust to dust. It left us feeling empty and raw and ever conscious of the energetic vacancy that my grandfather left in his wake. With Grandma, we were journeying through our first home death—something that felt both ancestrally familiar yet practically bizarre.

Rural North Carolina is a hard place to die. The closest on-call Hospice nurse lived over an hour's drive from our doorstep, the nearest in-patient facility was 90 miles away. We were isolated. Everyone was isolated. There was no funeral committee, no community to surround us and hold us close. Most people in this part of Appalachia die in the hospital in Asheville.

Few folks die at home in the way their ancestors did. Our neighbor up the road, an old lady named Bertha, nursed her adult son Billy at home as he died of cancer. I remember visiting their house when I was a kid and wondering why do so many people live in such a small space? Why is the ceiling covered in brown paper insulation backing? Why are all their hound dogs skinny like that? When Billy died, they turned down the AC unit in the window and drove to Bryson to get dry ice. I heard that his grave was dug by hand in the family plot out back.

In the city, they call this a "green burial." In Appalachia, they call it poverty, and as they say, "poverty is the best preservationist."

When Grandpa died in the hospice house in Asheville, my mother and I asked to wash his body. The nurse gave me a stunned, deer-in-the-headlights looks. "You actually want to do that?" she asked. But she put on a good show of looking for a wash basin and in the end, she provided some wet wipes.

In the early morning light, we took his long, cold arms out of his hospital gown. I pulled the little oxygen tubes from his nostrils. Mom gently took out his catheter while I tried hard not to look. We played some gentle Kirtan music on a little speaker and told Grandpa the story of his life. From forehead to foot, we washed him—singing, telling stories, and sending our prayers all the while.

When the time came to make decisions, Mom found the cheapest mortuary service Asheville could offer. "But they only have one star on yelp," she said incredulously. "Well, he's already dead. How bad can it be?"

The gentleman from the mortuary service looked like the Monopoly man. He had a spherical head, warm doughy hands, and fingers like sausages. His bedside manner was just as eerie. When he wheeled in the gurney, I didn't think a wheel could squeak so loud. The nurse was fiddling with the hospital bed controls, trying to make it the appropriate level. In a burst of annoyance, he took Grandpa by an arm and a leg and tried to hoist him onto the too-tall gurney single handedly. Another squeak. A literal dead thud. He dropped Grandpa's lifeless body onto the faux-wood floor. Mom let out a shrill cry and I fell into a fit of hysterical laughter.

*****

It's day eleven and reinforcement is coming. My college roommate is driving in from Asheville. Lyss is either a death tourist or a saint—probably both.

She calls me.

"Sweetpea, how are you?"

"I don't know."

"When was the last time you ate?"

"I don't know."

"Hang in there, Sweetpea—I'm on my way, and I'm bringing country cooking."

I put down the phone with shaky hands.

Lyss arrives with all the fixin's for macaroni and cheese, pork chops, collard greens, and fresh baked bread. My chosen sister. She who is a constant reminder that "the blood of the covenant is thicker than the water of the womb."

We eat and I can feel the stress melt out of the room. Lyss immediately takes control, delegating tasks and making a plan. Having been a caretaker for a young girl with severe disabilities, she has no problem coaxing Dilaudid into Grandma's mouth or teaching us how to change her diaper more efficiently.

Lyss' care allows for Mom and I to tend to Grandma's spirit. Tend to her altar. Call on our ancestors. Tell her the story of her life and hold her paper white hands. They are considerably cooler now.

Mom pulls out her old guitar—the one she's had since childhood—and plays old folk songs. Cash. Prine. Denver. Kristofferson. Peter, Paul, and Mary. All the legends Grandma had sung for us. Her fingers easily find the chords to the lullaby *Baby for Bobby*, as though they were waiting there to be played all along.

"And the wind will whisper your name to me.

Little birds will sing along in time.

Leaves will bow down when you walk by.

And morning bells will chime."

Our voices weave together over Grandma's supine body, her breaths growing further and further apart.

*****

Grandma was mostly vegetarian—she always said she wouldn't eat anything with a face. She picked this up at one of her new-age spiritual wellness retreats—Grandpa Jim called them her "junkets." For my eighth birthday, she gave me my first medicine drum made by an Ojibwe elder. Oak frame with horse hide. A pretty mare with a hawk feather braided into its mane was painted on it. She walked on hot coals in the front yard. She went days without eating or drinking while on vision quests in the woods. She drummed over friends so that they could find their spirit animal. She even built a sweat lodge next to the creek. I remember playing under its willowy frame during summer as a small child.

While at the Feather Pipe Ranch in Montana, Grandma was horrified to find a taxidermied moose head hanging on the wall of the main gathering lodge. When she inquired about why such a peaceful people would hang such a thing, she was met with a story of snow and sacrifice. Years ago, there was a grand blizzard and the road had been buried by an avalanche. People were stranded and the food stores were running low. The group met in that very gathering lodge to decide what to do, when a great moose approached with window. It threw its shaggy head back, bellowed to the heavens, and dropped dead. They knew it was a gift from the Creator—the sacrament of meat, the sacrifice of death. That moose meat kept them from starving until the roads were passable.

*****

It's day twelve and my uncle paces around Grandma's old one-room schoolhouse. His footsteps are shaking the floor beneath my feet. He's got a cigarette lit in his quivering hand and his bloodshot eyes are darting from me to the clothes splayed out across Grandma's bed.

"Didn't I do a good job laying out her clothes? I picked out only the light-colored ones. See? The white ones. And khakis. Wouldn't she look great in this shirt? It has a horse on it. She loves horses. What about this white skirt?"

I resist the urge to say, "Grandma wouldn't be caught dead in a skirt."

My uncle has been a lifelong junkie. From sixteen to fifty, he tried every drug known to man, and then some. His psyche was stuck somewhere between playful boy and dangerous teenager. I can recall a faint memory of barreling down the road in the backseat of the car as Mom drove him to the hospital. He had injected bleach into his veins. And he lived.

After a good bout with methamphetamine, the prodigal son has returned to see his mama through her transition. In her demented state, Grandma is overjoyed to have her boy finally home. His presence fills a decades old hole in her heart, and for that I'm grateful.

"These are great, right? Pick something out. Pick it out now."

He is trying to make up for not visiting Grandma as she's dying by facilitating my choosing of her clothing, which he's graciously pulled out of the closet and strewn across the room. Like a little boy, waiting to be told that he did a good job—his eyes plead for validation.

"Yes, that shirt is perfect. And how about the white linen pants?"

*****

It took thirteen days of active dying before our favorite on-call hospice nurse finally prescribed fentanyl. Grandma just could not pry her soul from her aching bones, and we wanted oh so desperately to ease her suffering.

I drove to the closest town with a pharmacy, but they didn't have something so menacing as fentanyl in stock. On the way out of the building, I ran into my middle school principal. He gave me a warm hug, took me by the shoulders, and walked me down the shampoo aisle—a serious furrow developing between his heavy grey brows. "Hannah, I've got to talk to you about something *really* important right now. I know your grandmother is dying, but is Barbara saved? Is she *truly* saved? Has she asked Jesus to be her lord savior? Have *you* asked him?"

Dear God. I think to myself. *This is insane. This is a nightmare.*

Lyss and I had to drive to the next town over to get Grandma's fentanyl. This is also the closest liquor store, the kind with the one-way doors and a separate entrance and exit. Walking down the bourbon wall, I had the feeling that we weren't the only ones packing opioids in that store.

When we got home, I offered to put the patch on Grandma's belly. The nurse had gone to see her next patient and I was anxious to not be my grandmother's mother anymore. I timidly pulled off the backer, remembering the many warnings and cautionary tales on the direction slips. Someone told me that getting some fentanyl under your fingernail was enough to kill you. I laid the translucent patch on her loose belly skin, just below her waistband.

Barbara Jean's jaw unclenched, and her fists unfurled. She stopped digging her heels into sheets. For the first time in twelve days, she let her knees part and her pelvis sink down into the hospital bed. Both of the cats jumped up and curled into the figure four of her relaxed legs. I could breathe again. We could all breathe again.

*****

The full moon hangs low in the still of the night. February is called the Snow Moon and it's as white as Grandma's alabaster skin. And probably just as cold. Her breaths are getting harder and fewer. Her eyes are distant and unseeing. She is gasping and we are praying. Soothe her. Sing to her. Ask for her safe crossing from the old gods and new. Look to your ancestors. Call on your angels. Witness every breath as though it was her last. Waiting.

It's just after midnight when she takes that final breath. That long, airy exhalation. Both immensely heavy and unbearably light. Her face sinks and it's just barely perceptible. Her eyes lose their luster and seem to wax over. There is a look of wonder to her mouth, a smile tinged with astonishment. There is a void where life once was.

*****

Ten minutes pass. And just like that, we get up—as though struck by some unseeable force. This is women's work. And it is time.

We tend to the windows first. All of them must be open. The wind rises outside. It makes the curtains dance and my heart flutter. We pull out our wash basin and three clean washcloths. Through a chorus of "I'll Fly Away," we smile upon Grandma and wash twelve days away.

We dress her in the white clothes my uncle had chosen. At first, we struggle with her dead weight, but we push on, singing. With the grace of a mother, we swaddle her in a makeshift shroud—mama's lace tablecloth. We place the owl feather on her chest and stand back, witnessing the fruits of our tending and care. This was women's work, oh we midwives of death.

The wind is still rising. It's streaming through the open windows. It's blown the candle out without being asked. On the windowsill, high above the living room there sits a little stuffed moose in a patchwork dress. It has sat there for years, gathering dust. As though Grandma herself has bumped into it, the moose falls to the foot of her bed, landing next to her shrouded knees.

It's as though Grandma was saying, loud and clear, "I've made it across that river, my loves. The sacrifice of my death will sustain your souls through the snowy winters of your life."

*****

We all slept lightly in the presence of the dead. I dreamt that I had gotten a sliver of fentanyl beneath my fingernail. In the nightmare, I died in my sleep like my friend's son when he overdosed on heroin. When I awoke from it, I couldn't go back to sleep for fear that I would forget to breathe.

The on-call nurse came in the early morning. She was gentle and kind and proper and reverent. When the mortuary service arrived, in waddled Monopoly Man.

Mom let out an exasperated sigh. We shared a look. As Mom hurled passive aggressive comments and the on-call nurse reassured her, the Monopoly Man wheeled his ever-squeaky gurney into the little log cabin. With a look of indignance, he let the nurse help him hoist Grandma onto it. It was a success.

Turning around with a look of triumph, the Monopoly Man bumped his big belly into the altar. The sound of a glass mason jar shattering inside the buskin bag told me that he had dropped Grandpa. Again.

Mom shrieked. The nurse cast aspersions. I broke down into the most hideous laughter the world has ever known.

*****

It's time for my high and mighty ruminations, but I won't tell you that death is anything close to bearable. From the sound of a death rattle to that very last airy exhalation, death is sublime agony. But we have access to tools, and ceremony is among them.

Ceremony is the lens my family and I used to view death from a sacred distance. And somehow, it made the pain a little more bearable, the irreverent laughter a little more reverent. It took the edge off. The grief. The gore. The sorrow. The smells. The family dysfunction. The great unknown. Ceremony made Grandma's death ok.

When we did it well. And, when we did it poorly. When we'd rehearsed it a thousand times. Or, when we made it up on the spot. When it came from the pages of some old book. Or, when it came from an ancient place inside us. When it was done at all, *ceremony* aided our dying matriarch in her pursuit of leaving a tired body and weary mind.

This I know in my bones.

Mom's Lift Off

Carol Hewitt

After Dad's death, Mom got a monkey dog. A funny looking small dog called a Brussels Griffin named Ringo. It didn't exactly replace Dad, but it helped with the loneliness of losing her lover and companion of 51 years.

In October of 1999, she had a plane ticket to visit us and was bringing Ringo. I was very much looking forward to seeing her.

And I was having one of the happiest days of my life.

I can't explain it. I just felt joyful. At one point, I checked the calendar to see what day of the month it was. Maybe this lightheartedness was hormones.

I thought back through the day. Had I drunk extra coffee? Eaten a lot of sugar? What else could be giving me this high? I felt so hopeful, so uplifted.

Mid-afternoon, I remember driving back from Chapel Hill. By now I had given up on figuring out the cause of this 'mood' and was trying to compare it to any way I had ever felt before.

The closest I could come up with was the feeling of being about two years old, when I hadn't a care in the world. Life was simply and deliciously pleasant, easy, relaxed, fun.

I pulled into the yard at about 5pm and got a call on my cell phone.

My brother David was on the line. He sounded terrible.

"Carol, I don't know how else to tell you this. Mom died today."

I was on such a cloud of bliss that his words landed softly, and my immediate concern was for my poor brother.

"Oh David, I'm so sorry. What happened?" I asked.

David frequently stopped by to visit Mom. On this morning, he found her lying on her side—knees tucked up, head resting comfortably on a pillow she had made with her hands, and eyes closed as if taking a nap. But this was 9:45am, and it was the bathroom floor, and she was wearing only her slip.

He tried to rouse her, but she was past asleep. As they say here in the South, she had already passed.

The rest of the details of the day are rough. He called 911 and they rushed over and tried to resuscitate her. Then took her to the hospital, and it was several hours before she was officially pronounced dead. Now David had the gruesome task of calling his four siblings who all adored her.

I consoled him as best I could and called my sister who lived in NYC. By some weird fluke, (that's if you don't give my mother the credit she's due for orchestrating things), Holly was only a few miles away, meeting with her one client in North Carolina.

I jumped in the car, and 30 minutes later we were sobbing together. Thank you, Mom.

Holly managed to get a flight home that evening, and I took her to the airport.

When I called the airline to explain that Mom had a ticket to visit me—but had died a few days before she could use it—they simply gave it to me to use to fly up to her funeral.

Mom had lasted just two years after Dad died. She was only 76. She died on October 22, four days before what would have been their 53rd wedding anniversary. I don't think she could face it or face another winter on her own.

That all sounds sad. But it was the most beautiful fall weekend. Her children came from across the country to be there. I hadn't been in New England in the fall for many years, having moved to North Carolina sixteen years earlier. It was spectacular.

She picked the prettiest time of year to die, and she passed right through me on her way out, or up, or whatever direction it was that she lifted off in. I felt it so distinctly all day. I now have an inkling of what it feels like to leave our physical body behind. It feels fabulous.

I am not afraid of dying. I need to clean my office first and write down where the heck everything is for the folks I will leave behind. But the dying part is fine with me.

I only hope I can give my loved ones the amazing gift Mom gave to me and pass through a few of them on my way out.

Aunt Sooz

Amy Parker

About 25 years ago—when I was 31 and recently separated from my husband—I found out during a visit home to my parents that my beloved aunt had breast cancer. After learning this information, I walked into my childhood bedroom, closed the door and dropped to my knees. Head against the side of the bed, I prayed—hard. With all I had, I begged G-d to not let her die. He didn't.

Last year, in 2019, the cancer came back. It took her in 3 unconscionably short months. By definition, it was a traumatic loss. Yet, surprisingly, I haven't been as bereft as I thought I'd be.

Do I miss her? I miss talking to her. I miss calling her and hearing her excitement and her sense of fun greeting me from the other end of the line. The joy of our aunt-niece relationship was that it always felt freeing to me. I had so much room to be *myself* with her. Within her palpable love for me, there was room for *me* just as I was. When I was with her, I felt like I was wonderful, clever and very lovable.

As a kid, I could be willfully, exasperatingly *impossible,* and still feel her love for me. She would just put me in my place, quickly and clearly, and her love for me would remain throughout the interchange.

The summer I was 12, she, my brother and cousins, were in the white Plymouth station wagon waiting for me.

The day was still hot, the blue plastic seats were sticky, and we were all going out to dinner. Very conscious of my appearance that summer, I was late because I had taken the time to successfully blow dry the curl out of my hair.

As I opened the door, I announced that everybody had to roll up the windows. Although I didn't say why, my aunt knew that I was worried that the wind and the humidity would make my hair all curly again. When everyone groaned, she turned around, looked at me with compassion, lightness and power, and said, "YOU have to get over yourself. Everyone, keep the windows open." And, even with such utter directness, her words didn't sting. They freed me. It *was* terribly hot. I leaned back and let my open window's rush of cool, pine needle-smelling wind take away my worries about my hair.

Her last months didn't go as I had wanted them to. When I heard her cancer had metastasized into her bones, and that she was choosing not to have treatment, I vowed to myself that I'd go home every weekend until she died. I would talk with her, tell her how much she meant to me, thank her for all she'd done, and have a really *good* goodbye.

That's not how it worked out. But there was a part of her death that was better than I could have ever imagined.

What I *had* imagined was that our trio—my aunt, my mom and I—would get to sit together and talk about the 50,000 things there were to go over, the territory that needed to be covered, before she died. We had *some* minutes like that, but not what I'd envisioned.

Everyone knew my aunt didn't have much time, so they were coming. Her brother from Colorado. Her son's best friend from childhood. Everyone. The room was always full when I'd arrive to visit her. I didn't want them to be taking up the precious little time I had to be with her, and, at the same time, didn't want to deprive them. So, I hung around, visited with people and worried there wasn't going to be time to really talk with her.

During the five hours it took me to get home, I was talking on the phone with a dear friend from college who had lost two of her sisters to breast cancer. I said I didn't know how I was *ever* going to be able to tell my aunt how much she meant to me or have the time to *even figure out* how to put it into words. My friend suggested, rather than try to carve out time I didn't have to write, whenever a wave of grief, or thoughts about her hit me, I could record those through my phone's voice memo app. I tried it one day and miraculously, as I talked into the app, I came up with a metaphor that made sense to me. Here's the voice memo I ended up emailing her:

Hey Aunt Sooz! It's Amy (voice cracking). *Oh, I might be a little teary. I was talking with a friend, an old friend from college, Barbara, the other day. Do you remember her? She was in my wedding—the one with the pretty, dark curly hair who (*laughing*) was wearing the dress that was really, really tight?—because she was an EMT in Kotzebue, Alaska, and didn't have any time or any place* *to have it fit, so she just put it on at the last minute, and then had to wear it that way.*

Anyway, I was talking to her today, and I was telling her how you have this stupid cancer in you. I was telling her I've been trying to figure out how to put into words what you've meant to me my whole life. She suggested I make a voice memo on my phone and send it to you.

So, I want to tell you that I was in Barnes and Noble this afternoon and I came upon some children's books. They were great books. They reminded me of you because they were books that celebrated kids' creativity. They were books about love and fun. They reminded me of all the fun we had, and how much you supported our creativity, whether it was our drawing, our reading of books, our running around—however we wanted to, or the plays we made at the lake.

Remember the summer Olympics and the gangster plays? That time when one of the boys, in hat and sunglasses, dramatically announced he'd stolen the "dough" and ran down the dock and fell in the water with the loaf of bread under his arm? Or the night we ended up turning the dishwashing into a scene from Oliver? We all walked across the long kitchen table with our pots, plates and towels while you led us in song?

(Starting to cry) *As I think about it now, a metaphor that makes sense to me is that, for me, you were kind of like the sun. I could always feel your love for me. So, whenever I was around you, even when I was being obnoxious or*

something, or when you had to tell me to get over myself,
I could still feel your love—kind of like the way I used to
feel the sun on my skin when I would lie on the dock
between you and mom.

I always felt the way you got a kick out of me, too.
Unlike the way I felt with other adults in our family who
loved me but were always trying to get me to be a bit
different, with you I felt that it was okay to be just how I
was. And I know you can imagine what a gift that was. I
know you get it, but I just want to tell you how grateful I
am for that because I think the love I felt from you helped
to protect the essence of me.

Okay. I love you. See you soon. See you when I get
there next week.

Keeping up with people as she did, my aunt checked
her email.

The next Saturday when I walked into her room, the
minute she saw me, she lifted her head, looked through the
crowd of people, and mouthed, with clear, deep
appreciation, "I got your email." Later, she said, with love
and loyalty, "Your mother deserves a lot of credit, too."

On the day she ended up dying, we were all sitting and
talking around my aunt's bed. She seemed unconscious. It
was time for me to go. I had an early morning flight home
the next day and my mother—who had been visiting my
aunt most every day for the last three months—was
exhausted. She needed to rest and have dinner. I felt this

stone-like weight on my heart because no part of my being wanted to leave, except I wanted to get my mother home.

It was time. So, I said, my heart breaking, "Aunt Sooz, we have to go now. I'm not sure if you'll see me in the morning. I wanted to be here with you when you go, but I have to fly home early tomorrow. I'm not sure what I'll do. Maybe you'll see me in the morning. I love you so much."

Then my aunt, who I thought couldn't hear anything, started to make these sounds. Huge sounds like she was trying really hard to communicate with me but just couldn't form any words. Her half-sister, gently putting her hand on Suzie's shoulder to comfort her, explained quietly to me, "hearing is the last thing to go."

I gave my beloved aunt a final hug, full of that my-heart-being-torn-from-hers feeling and walked out of the room. I said goodbye to the nurses and then, catching up with my mom, we walked shoulder-to-shoulder down the hallway of the rehabilitation center towards the door. I was deeply grateful for her presence. My mom, who had lived through the death of her parents and lately many of her dearest friends, had her mom-strength in place.

When I got to my parents' house, I borrowed their car and drove to my cousin's. He was my aunt's only son. He had been dealing with his mother's illness and care, his father's grief and his parents' estrangement.

When I got there, I joined him and his wife at their kitchen table. He poured me a drink. Over scotch, in those heavy-bottom glasses, I said, "Tonight would be a good night for her to die."

"You've just said what the rest of us are thinking," he said, appreciatively. We talked a bit longer and then, standing up, all 6 foot 4 of him said, "Come here. Let me show you something."

We went into his garage and he walked toward this deep blue, gorgeous little car. He called into his wife, "I'm going to take Amy for a ride." It was a beautifully built, smooth, and fast driving car.

We took it out to the highway. With the full moon straight out in front of us, keeping us company, he let out the engine. The speed took my breath away. It had a little of that crazy in it. The kind of crazy that makes sense when someone you love so much is dying.

The road graciously free of any cars at all so I could suspend worry about the speed and just listen as my cousin talked. With the moon keeping us company, and the highway clear, it felt deeply right.

He drove his beloved car fast. I was amazed by its beauty, its engineering, and its ability to soothe.

And, I was touched that he shared it with me.

We got back to their house. I said my goodbyes and drove back to my parents'. It was about 10:30 p.m. The minute I got there I said, "I'm driving back out to be with Suzie. I want to be with her if she goes tonight." My mom was surprised but respectful of my decision. "Okay, but don't you want anything to eat first?" I didn't.

Driving down Route 481, I was praying that she didn't die before I got there. If she was going to go, I wanted to be right there to keep her company. I didn't want her to have to be alone when she went; she had been there for me in so many ways, I wanted to be there for her.

I arrived at the rehab center, it was after hours so I had to wait for someone to open the locked door and let me in. I banged a bit on the door to get their attention. When I walked by the nurses' station, one of the nurses—the one who was really close to Suzie—was walking down the hall.

"She's in there. I just said goodnight to her about 5 minutes ago." I said, "Great. Thanks," and kept walking quickly towards her room.

I gave her a gentle kiss and said, "Hi Sooz." I sat down and took her hand. After about a minute or two, I noticed that she didn't seem to be breathing.

And then I had the most remarkable and previously unimaginable feeling. I felt her spirit nestle into the left side of my chest. It was like she moved right into my heart. She didn't leave me. She joined me.

I wasn't sad. I wasn't as bereft as I thought I'd be. Since she was with me in my heart, I felt this deep, deep comfort. And, honest-to-goodness, I've never felt like she left. I miss talking to her, and I often want to tell her things, but I don't feel without her—not even a whit.

As I think of it now, I'm not sure she could have put herself in any better place; she had moved into the *right* place for her safekeeping.

Unlike so many other important relationships, ours wasn't complicated. I didn't have any mixed feelings about the way we were towards each other.

I adored her, and she adored me.

My Beautiful Aunt Zillah

Gary Phillips

My Aunt Zillah died this week. She was my daddy's oldest sister.

There is a picture of her and my granny with the family cow, at age 13, taken in 1940. I like the way she fills out her overalls and how sullen she looks.

She was ever her own person and she loved me unconditionally, a comforting and always welcoming presence in my childhood.

Zillah was born into a share-cropping family and became a teenager between the Great Depression and the Great War. The Phillips' were so poor they sent their children to school without shoes, and Zillah worked like a man—sometimes plowing 14 hours a day behind a mule—until she was in her 30s. She and my dad were close in the way sometimes people are who have gone through very hard times together, and his eyes shone with a special light whenever she was around.

My Aunt Zillah had a great horselaugh, a way of throwing her head back, and raising her arms in hilarity or disgust. When she was serious, she was serious, and had intense heart-to-hearts with my momma, which resolved always into tears or belly laughs, both of which seemed to come from the same rich, abiding place.

One of the stars in the constellation of my life is missing, and I can feel a kind of loss of gravity, as I go about my life in a world that has so little to do with her or her experiences. Her final gift to me was the gift of tears, holding my broken-hearted mother in a little redneck Baptist church in the foothills, telling Aunt Zillah stories and working our patient healing way toward the belly laughs.

Writing Through Tears

Lyle Estill

Tami brought Chloe home as a puppy. His beard grew grey hanging out by my side.

After a lifetime together, he laid down by the back door and could no longer get up.

I published an entry in *Energy Blog* entitled, *Putting Chloe Down*:

Together we built trails, and passages, and ponds around the place. Together we hung around Summer Shop, sometimes with the burn barrel going. Chloe watched Summer Shop transform from sculpture to biodiesel to storage to living quarters. He wandered through them all....

Lisa arrived as the Angel of Death. She's the veterinarian that lives down the road. I held his knee, she found a vein, and injected an overdose with a pink syringe of anesthetic. Chloe didn't flinch. He didn't fight back. He looked up at me with dark eyes of relief, which I could barely see through my own tears.

When it was done, I wandered out to the fishpond. I could see Chloe swimming. He wasn't fond of water. He could take it or leave it. I pictured him as my vibrant companion—not as he was near the end.

He would have swum across the Hellespont if that were the way home."

*****

To my astonishment, *Energy Blog* lit up with comments. It appeared more people cared about Chloe's death than my thoughts on renewable BTUs. In those days, the phones in the control room never ceased. I would answer, "Piedmont Biofuels, this is Lyle, can I help you?"

There would frequently be a pause, followed by, "I'm sorry about your dog."

Our members, my readers, and those in our esoteric community of renewable energy reached out to comfort me. It was weird. I didn't know what to say. I missed Chloe, and I never meant to strike a nerve by telling the story of his death, but that essay ignited folks.

It was my first time writing through tears.

When my daughter Kaitlin was t-boned in a car crash outside of Ames, Iowa, I got the chance to do it again. Jaws of life. Helicopter rescue. Broken everything.

I got the news in a screaming phone call from her sister, Jessalyn. Next day, I moved into the Holiday Inn across from Mercy Hospital in Des Moines.

I wrote about it in a *Caring Bridge* website Jessalyn created:

Heart surgery successful. Brain hemorrhage. Go back three spaces.

Today she grabbed my hand.

When she approaches the edge of consciousness, her eyes open fully, and she looks at us without knowing who we are. She's not accustomed to seeing her mother and father together.

At the edge of consciousness, you can tell the pain moves in. She moans. And becomes agitated. She is strapped to the bed, with all manner of tubes coming and going. She makes complete sentences, like "I don't want a panda.

*****

I was terrified. I boarded the plane as an atheist, but there is no such thing at the bedside of a daughter in intensive care.

Comments poured in. Those from Ames skewed Christian. "The Lord is with you." Those from Pittsboro skewed pagan. "Sending good energy." I could feel them all. I could feel prayers coming down the hospital hallway.

My daughter Jessalyn wrote, "Dad was startled by two new wires spotted going into her head but was relieved to find they were simply coming from her hot pink iPod."

Kaitlin went on to a full recovery. When she walks into the room today, she's beautiful, and smart, and powerful again.

Not so with my brother Mark. Months by his bedside resulted in death from "Never Smoker Lung Cancer."

Mark was spousal to me. He was my protector. My mentor. My best friend. We talked several times a day on the phone, went to lunch constantly, and frequently chopped wood on weekends. When he died, he blew an inexorable hole in my life.

At his end, my job was to hold him down when he came-to. Whenever he gained consciousness, he ripped away at the tubes on his arm, and the tube on his penis, as anyone would. I would hold him down until the orderly could increase his sedative. It was the first time I was stronger than my big brother Mark.

The night Mark sent me to his house to fetch his living will was the night I walked through molten lava. Tears splashed on the keyboard as I wrote about Mark's final days. I had a riveted audience. Again.

By the time I sprung Mark from UNC Hospital and got him into his hospice bed at home, he was beyond speaking. His eyebrows had fallen off and his bald head was covered in scabs. He shot me a "high sign" of gratitude by lifting his arms above his head as if he had just scored a goal in hockey. Mark was proud of having played hockey in every decade of his life.

He died a few hours after being home, as I was perusing his cupboards and thinking about all the healthy meals I was going to make for him.

I wrote Mark's obituary for the New York Times— his beloved daily.

*****

Days later I wrote in *Energy Blog*:

Counting the Hours

My high school buddy John Dodd wrote me from Minnesota. He says it takes 100 days for your head to clear.

I went to work today. Day 6 without Mark in the world.

I went to staff meeting, and I did some time in the Control Room. I shoveled out of some messages, and I told a customer that Mark had passed.

I made some rotten comments, and I scared the daylights out of some really good folks, and I wish I would have stayed in bed. I'm hoping no one on-project listens to me for 30 days.

I picked up my boys—Arlo and Zafer—around noon and came home despondent. Frank's truck was parked at Summer Shop.

He had shot a doe in the orchard and was kind enough to let me watch him clean and dress it. I shed my office wear, eagerly climbed into ratty clothes, and jumped in. It was a wonderful distraction. He gutted, and skinned, and butchered the deer, while I watched and learned and tried to help. And when he left, the fridge was full of fresh deer meat.

I gave him a handful of white potatoes—the last of the season, that Jack had brought by. Then I went out and harvested some mistletoe from the river birch by the pond.

Frank gets some mistletoe and potatoes. I get a fridge full of meat. I joked with the boys that everyone brings food by the house in a time of mourning. Frank's just happened to be on the hoof.

But what I really received was the afternoon off. The distraction was everything. No decisions. Which was good. Since I am having a hard time finishing sentences and thoughts.

Just when I think I will be able to get back on the horse which is my life, an aunt calls from afar, or my brother Jim fires off an email, and I find myself right back in the mud.

Tonight, Arlo and I drove to Ray's General Merchandise and picked up four pounds of fat from the back of the meat counter—along with a bunch of white butcher paper. We are going to turn this deer into sausage and ground venison and steaks.

It's not something I have ever done. But it will be better than counting the hours without Mark...

*****

I missed Mark. Pittsboro missed Mark. My mom and dad and brothers missed Mark. His death was a blow from which none of us ever recovered.

Like Mark, my father suffered a horrible death from cancer. His was pancreatic, liver, and "everything else cancer."

The diagnosis stunned us. Dad was a teetotaler who had spent a lifetime on carrot sticks and fitness. It was shocking to hear he was shot through with certain death. I turned to writing poetry:

Short Time

Dad was a wrestling fan
I wrestled
He came to every meet

My sons wrestled
I went to almost every match

As a fan, Dad sat silently in the crowd
As a dad I screamed my lungs out
Three two-minute periods:

The first won with technique
the second won with conditioning
the third won with heart

When my sons were in trouble
on their backs, fighting the pin
I would watch the clock
and scream out the time

When they would hear "short time"
from their father
they would fight a few seconds longer
for the period to end
to get out of trouble
to begin again

Now my dad is dying
He's on short time
And me?
I don't know what to scream...

*****

Dad and I got right before he died. He was proud of me, and I loved him deeply. We had managed to set our differences in the outer parking lot, and had found connection through children, and family, and business. He was a hero of mine. Here is part of a letter I wrote to him:

Dear Dad,

I was really glad to see you on my recent trip to Canada. When you lost your interest in eating, I thought maybe the end was near, and I wanted to see you before you embark on your final journey.

One of my regrets in life is my last sight of Mark—which still haunts me. I remember you driving through the night, arriving at the hospital, and I remember how I stopped you before entering ICU to say, "Steel yourself."

As you know, the Mark you said goodbye to in no way resembled the man you thought you were coming come to see. I didn't want that to happen again, so I drove up to have a final memory of you as you are now. "Grandpa as usual," as Zafer would say.

When we sprung you from the hospital, you had lost some weight. I remember feeling your spine when we hugged goodbye. At the time, I thought that might be our last visit together—but you went ahead and turned "months" into over a year. And here we are.

And while I am grateful for our last couple of visits, I didn't really know what to say. As is often the case with me, when I am lost, I turn to books. Mom slipped me a copy of Maggie Callanan's Final Gifts: A Practical Guide for Bringing Care and Comfort at the End of Life when I left your place on my recent visit.

Callanan was a hospice nurse for many years, and her book is filled with real world examples of people and families on the edge of death. It's a wonderful read, filled with clarity and insight—if you don't mind bawling your eyes out while you read.

It dawned on me that I have a history of crying while reading on airplanes. I bawled all the way to Des Moines when Kaitlin had her accident, and I remember how everyone—from TSA flunkies to taxi drivers—seem to make way for a crying father. Shortly after Mark died—on a trip home from New York—I waded into James Taylor's Letters to Stephen, also given to me by Mom. It tore me apart. *I shared the plane with the off-Broadway cast of High School Musical—dancers and singers coming to Durham to put on a show, and as I recall my tears subdued their boisterous party.*

Callanan talks about "dying right." We put a lot of energy into living right. We strive to work smarter. We study living. But when it comes to dying right, we don't even know where to begin.

I think you are dying right. I'm proud of you for swearing off treatments and for preparing to die at home, with Mom and all of us able to visit. The gap between your prognosis and your final day has allowed so many of the people who love you to express their thoughts—whether it is letters from your former employees or visits from grandchildren.

I laughed when I heard you had cancelled a recent teeth cleaning—not wanting to have the cleanest teeth in the cemetery. Nice work.

None of which changes the fact that I wish I had read Final Gifts before my last visit. It's one thing to talk about the World Series as we did. Quite another to talk about your death.

I'm guessing you are awfully sick of dying by now. I wonder if it bores you terribly. You don't like being mollycoddled. And you don't like hanging around in bed. As a lifelong man of action, I'm guessing this period of your life must drive you crazy. I wish I could have asked you about that.

When I departed for Canada, Arlo said "You do know what every dad wants, right?"

"What is that?" I replied.

"Every dad just wants their son to be proud of them," he said.

Funny, Arlo. I think that is supposed to be the other way around. But maybe he is right. I'm proud of you. I think you are dying right, and I regret not having had the words to say that when I was sitting across from you in your living room.

Just as I turn to books when I am lost and confused, I also turn to this keyboard to find solace when I am in a fog.

Something Callanan did not say—but I think might be true—is that grief seems to be cumulative. Reading her wonderful stories of palliative care evoked memories of Kaitlin's accident, and Mark's death, and summoned memories of you at every turn of the page. Each short chapter is rather like a punch in the solar plexus...

*****

Dad always showed up for his boys. I was doing a book tour that included a stop in Guelph, Ontario. He was freshly released from the palliative care ward, with ankles so swollen that he attended the reading in his bedroom slippers. Dad was proper. You wouldn't generally find him in public in his slippers. But he showed up. He always showed up for me.

Dad starved himself to death. Euthanasia had not yet come to Canada. We treat our pets better than our parents when it comes to end of life. Chloe was lucky. My brothers—Jim and Glen—did the heavy lifting at the end of Dad's life. All I had to do was cry and drive for days to get to his living room to say goodbye.

Mom asked me to write his obituary. I remember her editing it severely.

My son Zafer wore Dad's wingtips to Dad's funeral. He went on to wear Dad's sweaters and Dad's golf shirts.

Until he died from a heroin overdose.

When Zafer died we were knocked into another orbit. We held a rager that lasted for weeks and staged a service half the size of the town. A committee took over our house. Refrigerators were installed on the porch. Every meal was a meal for dozens. Kegs of beer arrived and were replenished.

I wrote prolifically. And sobbed convulsively. Comments and sharings poured in faster than we could comprehend them. To this day, folks I barely know comment on how grateful they were for my writings on the death of our son. Somehow, I managed to galvanize grief with writing, the whole time crying my eyes out. One of my entries was titled *Grave Digging Time*:

Years ago, when Tami and I dabbled in real estate, I always thought a graveyard would be the perfect entrance to a development.

I figured the demographics were with us. And I thought human remains might make a nice buffer from encroaching sprawl. Where I grew up, we used to play in graveyards all the time. They were green spaces. With sweet monuments to hide behind and climb upon.

I was supposed to build a graveyard here, at the Burrow, where we live. Our neighbor Chris is dying from ALS, and he needed a place to be buried. I mapped out an idea—a low impact trail from one driveway to another, which could be dotted with gravesites and tombstones along the way. I was supposed to get together with Chris to pick out a gravesite for him.

Not sure why I didn't get around to that one. I did walk up to his place one day to get him on board. But I couldn't bring myself to go to the door. I wasn't sure what to say.

"Hey, Chris. How are you doing, man? What do you say you get in your wheelchair and we go pick out a place for us to bury your body when you die?"

Afterward maybe we could go back to his place, have a few beers and watch the game.

That all changed when Zafer died. All of sudden, people need to know how they wanted me to ship my son's body. One moment my world is over. The next it needs attention. The next it is surreal. It's at once terrifying, confusing, and filled with fear.

Bob and Joe marked out a low impact trail. Trip made it happen with his Bobcat. Instant graveyard. Check.

Tami and I walked up there this morning to select a gravesite for Z. Lexie arrived with lattes from town. The morning light slipped through the pines and a bunch of us wandered the new trail. Tami was impressed. Happy to know our son's body would have a home there.

With a green light from Tami, all we needed was a grave. Arlo pulled in with our little backhoe. I walked up with a shovel. He did most of the work. I admired his fluidity at the controls given the tears running down his dusty face. I snatched a holly tree from the site and transplanted it down at our house. My brother Glen pitched in. So did Joe. In no time we had a grave dug for Zafer. Check.

I was walking home with a spade over my shoulder when I fell apart.

I passed Chris's porch. He was sunning himself in the cool April breezes. He's lost his ability to speak, but that doesn't matter. He had been quietly observing our comings and goings, and he was bawling his eyes out. I grabbed a chair, sat down next to him, and held his hand.

I told him about how I had been remiss on consulting with him on his gravesite. We talked about how he was supposed to go first. In between my sobs, he transcribed messages onto his phone. We actually had a few laughs.

When I arrived at our house, I grabbed a bucket of water and schlepped it up to the newly transplanted holly tree. As I watered it, I thought that perhaps it would live. And prosper. Put out berries for the birds. Be biologically successful.

Which reminds me. I need to take it another bucket today. As the horror begins anew.

*****

When Zafer died I lost all interest in writing, and speaking, and public readings. I immersed myself in painting, portraiture, drawing and the creation of my sixth book—a graphic biography about Zafer's life entitled *Memoir for Margot.* Good thing I moved into visual art, since we don't even have a word for a parent who has lost their child.

Shortly after Zafer's death, my marriage to Tami also changed. Our struggle to continue as a couple morphed into my moving in with Lexie for over a year. Lexie held me while I sobbed, but I never wrote a word of it. It was as if I couldn't handle any more writing through tears.

Until my mom died.

My brother Jim stopped in on her one Saturday morning and found her dead on the bathroom floor. My brothers decided I needed to write Mom's obituary. Glen called me with the news.

For the first time in years, I had a writing assignment. I snuck out to Bull McCabe's, an Irish pub in Durham, pulled up a seat at the bar, and started writing a "goodbye" to my mother. I had a beer and tried to write as I sobbed.

Some guy came up beside me, in that dark Irish Pub, and said, "Wow, are you able to write in public?"

I turned to him with tears burning my cheeks and explained that I was attempting to write a eulogy for my mom. I thought that would get rid of him.

I was wrong. He was from West Virginia. Just moved to Winston-Salem. Had to get away.

Nice guy. My crying retreated as I listened to his random story. He picked up a platter of shots and vanished into the bar.

I turned back to my writing. The Guelph Mercury is out of business. They can't publish this obituary. Mom wouldn't want the New York Times. The brothers agreed that the platform was Facebook.

I posted *Burying Annie*:

...Mom was an intellectual. She loved to read. And to learn. She told stories. And loved the arts. From her I received the gift of gardening. And bird watching. From Mom I learned about theatre. And radio.

She loved CBC radio. I remember her crying as she ironed and listened to the news in 1968 when Bobby Kennedy was shot. I was playing with her spools of threads beneath the ironing board.

Ann was a homemaker. A stay at home Mom who kept her boys in homemade cookies. She mended socks. Picked out wallpaper. Submitted recipes to Gourmet magazine. And she raised her boys with a linen fist. Mom refinished furniture. Stenciled old things. She revered "stuff" from the past and kept a close eye on her ancestors.

She was a keeper of photo albums, a maker of scrapbooks, and a writer of memoirs.

Mom buried her firstborn son, my brother Mark. And she buried her husband Don—who shared a bed with her for 61 years. She also buried her grandson, Zafer.

At Zafer's memorial she came out on stage as a doddering old woman. But once she was at the podium, she laid it down. Like she always did. She was a deep introvert with a vast intellect that could spit wisdom when needed.

Lover of poetry. Lover of nature. Lover of family.

I had a wonderful conversation with her the day before she died. I had her laughing. She would call it "being in stitches..."

*****

I finished my post and tried to settle my tab. It was picked up by the stranger from West Virginia. It turns out writing can buy beer.

My rational brain understood that Mom had a good run. Her eyesight was failing. Her hearing was failing. Her mobility was reduced. Mom was lonely without Dad. She went in turn. Everything was "right" about her death. She didn't need to starve herself. Her eyebrows didn't fall off. Mom died the way we all want to die.

And yet my lizard brain still felt like I was riding the tail of an enraged Tyrannosaurus Rex.

Now that both of my parents are dead, I can't decide if I am an adult or an orphan. I don't want either mantle. I don't want to be the dead kid's Dad. I want my brother Mark to be back in my corner. I don't want them all to be gone.

As always, I return to the keyboard:

Walking Again

On the chiropractor's bench I
put my faith in the sound of
a cracking bone.
I hobbled to lunch with an old friend
who said: "You couldn't walk when
your father died either."

I'll be damned
I had forgotten that.

All I have to do
now that Mom is gone
is learn how to walk again.

The Privilege of Grief

Tami Schwerin

If someone told you that your life would be amazing and brilliant—full of adventure, love, excitement, creativity, scandal, drama, and privilege, with a few ups and downs, but extraordinary overall—what would you say?

There is one caveat.

You will lose one of the most precious things in your life. You will make the biggest sacrifice. And you won't know what it is or when it will happen.

You might say yes. If you didn't know any better.

Evidently, my son Zafer and I made that deal long before either of us were born. We had a contract, and because we both needed to learn some lessons on a soul level, we said, "Sure, that would be awesome."

I had a most beautiful life. A fabulous family with two sons and two stepdaughters that all loved each other deeply. If they chose to be with anyone, it was with each other. Blended families don't always have that, but we did.

We were that family that everyone envied. Our vacations, our gatherings, our lifestyle, and our challenges. They called us the "Kennedy's of Pittsboro." The children that were "embarrassingly beautiful" my mother-in-law would say. She stopped showing pictures to her friends because she didn't want them to feel bad.

*****

April 14, 2016 was a beautiful spring evening. I heard a loud knock on the front door at midnight. I lifted my head and woke my husband, Lyle. I could see the entire back of the house lit up eerily through the windows.

We both went to the front door and there was a sheriff, his spotlights lighting the whole place up. He asked if I was Tamela Schwerin. I confirmed. He started asking about our son Zafer. My younger son, Arlo, drove Zafer's beat up truck and I thought maybe he was in trouble. He must have gotten a ticket or something. I didn't want Arlo awakened and I was pissed at the sheriff. I started putting my hands up as a protective measure, *don't get near my son.*

But he kept saying Zafer's name.

I was sure he was mistaken, and I just kept getting angrier. And then, I saw Lyle crumple to the floor. I finally heard the sheriff say that Zafer Estill had died and he was at the coroner's office in Boulder, Colorado. In my magical thinking, I thought—*oh, we can fix this. No problem. I'll get to work on this, and it will all be ok.*

Lyle asked through his wailing how Zafer had died, and the sheriff said he had smoked heroin.

We had never considered heroin a thing, much less something that could be a threat to our child. When I was growing up, heroin was something older people did with needles under a bridge, maybe in New York City or somewhere. I had never talked to my kids about heroin.

Lyle called Zafer's roommate. She was distraught and said, yes, this was true. Our night of hell began.

Lyle wailed and screamed outside. I didn't want to wake Arlo and tell him that his hero, his big brother was no longer on this earth. I wanted him to have a few more hours of bliss.

I just couldn't believe it and was in a wild state of shock. I couldn't cry. The time went by so slowly. I would look at the clock and it never seemed to move. I looked in the mirror to try and make sense of what was happening, and my face was stuck in a look of horror; I looked like the painting of The Scream. But I couldn't scream and couldn't cry.

Arlo woke up and came down the hall. I asked him to sit down. He sensed something awful had happened. I just said that Zafer had smoked heroin, and it had killed him. I grabbed him to protect him as he writhed in pain. I didn't want him to hit his head on the table. I tried to hug him tight to keep his pain manageable. Which was impossible.

We spent the next few hours walking around like zombies. Finally, the three of us got in our king size bed and held hands, and I just prayed for the sun to come up. It seemed like days before it did. Lyle and Arlo finally fell asleep for a minute as the light came through the window. I got up to make calls in the front yard where I could get cell coverage. I didn't know what to do, and I didn't want to utter those words. *Zafer died.* That was incomprehensible. That couldn't have happened.

I called my brother-in-law to ask him what to do, and he said I had to tell people. I called my dad and asked him to drive to my mother's and tell her that Zafer had died. I thought that I would be all alone in trying to figure this out and to deal with it. My neighbor found out and called, hysterically, "What can I do?" She was a second Mom to Zafer and an attorney, so I asked her to get him home.

People started driving up. Neighbors were walking through the woods. Friends and family began calling. People were getting on planes from Paris, California, Colorado, Pennsylvania, and New York. They started driving from Canada, and Florida, and Washington D.C. Everyone was coming to help us.

Someone gave me a Valium. I'm not into pharmaceuticals, but this was appropriate technology, and I'm grateful. It helped me get through, minute by minute, and hour by hour. I fell asleep and awoke to a living room of standing-room-only friends and family. There was this sense of surrealism. Some days, it is still there. *How could this be happening? This can't be happening.* Being surrounded by everyone was a huge comfort. I don't have to do this alone. The love and pain on their faces helped me.

We started putting the pieces together about what happened. There were conversations with the police, the coroner, and Zafer's sweet roommates. We needed to communicate to the public. Plan a ceremony. Bury Zafer. And, of course grieve and understand.

Alisa, my neighbor whose husband was dying of ALS, created a huge altar on our porch which quickly filled with photos, letters, candles, and mementos. It became a source of comfort and made us laugh and cry.

We didn't think about it at the time, but the whole family was honest about how Zafer died. Many families keep this cause of death hidden for lots of reasons. There may be shame involved. Or investigations. Or levels of privacy. We all felt that it could help others to know what happened. Zafer made a huge mistake that continues to ripple out, and we didn't want others doing the same. There was never a sense of shame about Zafer. My beautiful stubborn, brilliant boy made a terrible mistake. Heroin is one of the most addictive substances in the world. I had never heard about the opioid epidemic.

*****

Zafer had a mind of his own from the day he was born. He and I spent idyllic days together in the woods of Chatham County, feeding chickens and collecting eggs. I hiked trails with Z in a baby backpack. I couldn't bear to hear my baby cry and would take him into our bed. Lyle wanted our bed back, so he tried to "ferberize" him, a process of self-soothing. Lyle would sit on the roof outside the window near Zafer's crib and smoke cigars. He turned up the stereo loud, so I couldn't hear his cries. But after a couple of days, Zafer was back in our bed again.

Zafer grew up and he knew there was something different about our family. He was embarrassed that our cars smelled like French fry grease and our driveway was a half mile long. We didn't have a TV, and his friends at school believed hurricanes were caused by God.

Z grew into a stubborn and ambitious young man. He wanted to conquer the world. He had big vision, and he set a high bar for his friends and family. He loved to travel, and if we said "no" to expensive plane tickets, Zafer would find a way. He would call us from some fancy pool in Florida on spring break. "How did you get there, Zafer?" I would ask. "Don't worry about it, Mom," he would say with a mischievous laugh.

The boy got so many speeding tickets that our entire family's insurance was canceled. I called him to scold him the night he died. He said "Mom, I'm allowed to be young and reckless. I'm going to call GEICO." I couldn't help but laugh at my beautiful charming son. He said I love you and I told him I loved him. Our last words.

*****

Seeing the community come to our aid the week of Zafer's death was a miracle. We were not the only ones devastated—the entire community was. Even people that didn't know Zafer were affected. We heard stories of how the loss of Zafer caused people to make life changes. Some moved away and followed their dreams. Some marriages broke up because life is too short. Some made drastic changes in their lives. We will never be the same. His action caused tidal waves.

A support team formed organically as friends and family came to be by our side. Twenty people, affectionately known as "The Committee," put their lives on hold for over a week to help feed and clean and prepare for a massive funeral. They held conference calls, made spreadsheets, and used their vast talents to organize the meals, the booze, the housing, the communications, the transportation and whatever else was needed. We essentially held a ten-day wake.

Our neighbor Camille, an avid homesteader and vegan, was in charge of food donations. One of my dear friends from high school who is now an IBM executive called to offer help. Camille took the call and said, "can you be in charge of dinner tomorrow night?"

"Sure," Jane said. "What do they like?"

"Meat, they like meat."

"What kind of meat?" Jane asked.

"Squirrel. Squirrel for 75, please."

I think Jane dropped the phone at that point.

The community loaned cars, did airport runs, and opened up their houses for out-of-town guests to stay. Many of those friendships continue today. Because we were part of the local food movement, the farmers and restaurants sent farm-fresh food to our house. The local NPR affiliate even brought in a case of wine. Others hauled kegs and cases of champagne.

Our house is surrounded by forest and cantilevered over a pond with a huge deck and a rope swing. The woods became dotted with tents and RV's to house the college kids that came to support our children. There were dozens of people—young and old alike—painting toenails, getting massages, playing music, singing, swimming, crying and laughing. It was one of the most incredible feelings—to be surrounded by so much life and joy, and the deepest sadness at the same time. I've never felt so supported. It was a bubble of pure love.

Our family sat together and agreed on the service that would honor our Z-boy. We put together a list of music, poetry, speakers, and pall bearers. We were learning about green burial, so we just stated what we wanted, and the vast network made it happen.

We decided to use Zafer's beloved beat up little biodiesel "pup" truck to drive him, in a locally made pine box, to the burial ground. There was some controversy.

Would the coffin fit, or would we have to drive with the tailgate down? What if he fell out of the back? Was it legal? Can his brother and sister legally drive him to his final resting spot, the graveyard we built on our land? Would we need permits?

The answer was simple. It's all legal and whatever we wanted we could have. The worst possible thing had just happened, and we were able to put Zafer and ourselves first.

Together, we created one of the most moving events of all time. Hundreds came to the service. Our entire family spoke. I don't know how we did it, but we were all able to stand and deliver a eulogy. About twenty of Zafer's friends accompanied him and placed his casket lovingly on the stage to say their goodbyes. A wooden "Z" was carved and put on his pine casket. We sat down to Pink Floyd's "Wish You Were Here." We all sang Leonard Cohen's "Hallelujah" as we walked out. *Your faith was strong, but you needed proof.*

Arlo, his sister, and his best friend drove the beat-up Pup carrying Zafer's body behind the police escort. Hundreds of cars followed as we drove the 8 miles to our graveyard. It started to rain. The police were at all the major stoplights to make sure we didn't have to stop. The town came to a standstill for Zafer. The Pittsboro police switched off with the county sheriffs as we hit the town line. The sheriffs escorted us the rest of the way in a perfect ballet.

We brought Zafer to his resting place in the forest. His grave was dug by his brother, dad, grandfather, uncle, and closest neighbors. We gathered, said a few more words, sang Amazing Grace, and lowered him into the hole. I started putting dirt on my son's coffin. I wanted to keep going, but someone gently pulled me back. The community took turns with six shovels, covering him up. It was awful but seeing the pain and determination on everyone's faces helped me to know I wasn't the only one hurting. Someone kept singing until he was completely buried with dirt. There was a comfort, like we were putting a blanket on Zafer.

We walked back to the house and there was a feast prepared for everyone by the local restaurants, farmers, and friends.

The next day, most of our guests returned to their homes, their jobs, and their lives. That was the beginning of my journey of healing and awakening. It will last a lifetime.

*****

I am privileged to have been taken care of by this community.

Back in 2006, I founded a non-profit called Abundance NC. Our mission was to educate folks about local food, renewable energy, and resilient community. Zafer's death gave me a whole new perspective. The community became most important.

After Z's death, my staff and board of directors took over so that I didn't have to go back to work for some time. I was incapable of being functional. My brain couldn't figure out very simple things. Trauma like this has been compared to a car accident where your head goes through the windshield. But you look fine, so people don't get it. It takes a very long time to heal, but research shows that you can heal from emotional trauma, and that your brain can actually expand.

The first year was a complete shock for me. The second year was one long realization that what had happened was true. And after the third anniversary of losing Zafer, I began to step out of the fog. I'm still working on it.

I have tried every healing modality: psychics, somatic healing, channelers, séances, massages, acupuncture, and chiropractic. From reiki to sound healing. I have been to workshops and talk therapy. I've journaled and gone on solitary retreats. I've written blogs about Zafer. I've talked with other mothers who have lost their children. I've climbed mountains, sat under waterfalls, and faced some of my fears. I've held rituals. I've keened and wailed, which helped move the grief the most. I've held three birthday parties for Zafer. I even threw a masquerade ball for him.

The night the sheriff knocked on the door, I was reading a book about death and grief. The staff of our little non-profit had talked about putting on a Death Faire because my neighbor was dying of ALS. I decided that we couldn't actually put on the Death Faire now—I felt like I had manifested death.

It was a small town. When my husband and I would go out in public, we would notice that people were scared of us. We had a lot of horrible experiences with people either running from us or saying exactly the wrong thing. And I would have *been* one of those people only months earlier.

I decided that I *had* to put on a Death Faire. I had to create an event that brought together grief educators, green burial vendors, workshop leaders, poets, artists, musicians, and the leaders of the conscious death movement—to forge a community of healing. We built an altar in the very center of Death Faire for remembering our loved ones. With the help of so many people, we created the most diverse, meaningful event we have ever held. Six hundred people showed up to an event that many believed would be strange, sad, and scary. But death is the common denominator. It brings people together. Now, we are planning our 4th Annual Death Faire and people look forward to the event year-round.

So do I.

I am learning to be grateful for the 19 years I got to have with my son. I am a different person than I was before and deeply thankful for my continued awakening. Love never dies. Never.

We hold Death Faire around All Soul's Day when the veil between the world of the living and of the dead is the thinnest. Strange occurrences always happen around this week. It's when I truly feel Zafer and the other spirits of those I have known. It is as if they are cheering us on.

I will always be proud of Zafer, and I imagine he is proud of me.

i want to undie you

Jaki Shelton Green

i have come to this new place whose trees have no
medicine
barren ground that has never tasted a thimble of blood
where birds fly backwards and sky is afraid of falling
it is here that i say goodbye to my woman-child who is
remembering her true name and searching for the river
where her story was born

the woman-child climbs hills that scratch her without
mercy
she becomes the balm for the angry ground that refuses to
see her
without country she becomes the map of all her ages
without eyes she becomes the compass of her own heart

i hear her offering sacrifices to the ocean the wind to the
fires of her uncertainty
not now spirit wails
not now

spirit carves patience grace tenderness inside her palms
between her ribs
the lost ones wait for her
the ones she's been waiting for
pale ghosts running from their own shadows
she is the one they've been waiting for

death is not enough for you my woman-child

it will not feed the dry season in your throat
it will not water the parched soles of the ones who came
before you
it is not even the theater you've dressed for

the trees cry out for your medicine
this earth does not need your breath
the earth needs your hands planting and watering new
seeds

this place needs the medicine inside your hands
your clan waits for the feast you have prepared for this
season of harvest
choose red vibrant pulsating knives that go gently into
your bread of life

the trees have no song
muted by ghosts who trod dragging skeletons
dragging undergrowth dragging swords of a sun-bleached
confederacy

any road traveled any room any door any window courting
the wafting breeze of lemon balm jasmine rosemary
cypress all lead back to you sweet woman-child first born
first death of your mother's heart
the hands of a village draw invisible smoke circles of
myrrh frankincense cedar around your hospice house this
sweet house wrapping you in new skin for new dreams that
weave new story

we gather with open unclenched palms we gather all the markings of your tribe who you were before you were born and who you are now becoming as you once again travel towards the river where blood is born

wings of flight and tenderness for this
unknown sky
the spirits of mothers grandmothers fathers and grandfathers spoke to you through the last rain you'd ever smell hear feel taste

the hands of our womb tribe gently caressed your skin still warm
it contained another breath that we felt under our hands as we washed your body oiled your crevices valleys your cheeks flushed with smile

the people of many villages gathered to hold me
they came with food flowers holy water words open hearts unnamed strangers gathered at your gravesite unnamed faces and familial faces cried a river of tears as we gently unraveled the strings of our hearts releasing you and your new wings into a new sky
people bring stories of you to me written on linen rags befitting for your nights of rescuing lost desperate souls your nights of sharing food offering a bed offering a sanctuary for affirmation

people bring stories of you to me written inside the coat sleeves of a battered coat that is so alive with the language of sorrow you can hear the coat whispering a coat that used

to be purple is now all the colors of nights gone bad nights
without light or shadows

people bring stories of you to me wrapped with sharp
precision inside blank envelopes that tremble with all the
stories its carried these stories wet with the breath of rivers
where you've jumped in to save the teenage girl when other
suicides weren't enough for her

people bring stories of you to me in shiny
glass bottles where you live as their genies of hope but
they've forgotten the magic words that might bring you
back they hold on to the bottles where you've helped them
tuck their dreams for safe passage

people bring stories of you to me in bright colored pyrex
dishes steaming hot with their memories of your own open
festive table brimming with soulful vibrant food that fed
their souls deeper than their bellies your recipes of ancient
healing crawling inside shattered spines crushed limbs
reviving diseased hearts

people bring their stories of you to me inside baskets
woven so tight they hold the tears of four generations of
torn women their skirts stained hands knees bruised cut
they bring stories of your arrival to their village no secret
potions no magical creams or oils only you with wide
open face wide open spirit and the needles of sisterhood
helping them stitch the shawls of balm for their unborn
generations

i want you to un-die. come back said the mother.

i want you to undie. i want the dust of you un-scattered. i
want the hush of you un-hushed. i want the cries for you
un-cried. i want you to un-die. i want the tomb of you un-
tombed. i want the dirge of you un-sung. i want the grief
of you un-grieved. the clock of you
un-stopped. the length of you un-folded. i want the scars
of you un-scarred.
i want the road of you un-traveled. i want the fret of you
un-fretted. the prayers of you un-prayed. i want the scream
of you un-screamed.

i want the verb of you un-verbed. i want the slumber of
you un-slept.
i want the shroud of you un-shrouded. i want the earth of
you un-broken. the river of you un-flowed. the desert of
you un-barren. i want to un-morning *that morning*. i want
to un-break the broken of you. i want to un-confuse the
confusion of you. un-diagnose the diagnosis of you. un-
steal the stolen of you. un-murder the murdered of you. un-
butcher the butchered of you. un-wound the wounded of
you. un-bound the bondage of you. un-sterilize the sterility
of you. un-deny a life denied to you. un-seal the sealed of
you. un-mask the masks of you. un-veil the veils of you.

un-expose the exposed of you. un-sacrifice the sacrifice of
you. un-erase the erasure of you. un-lock the locked of
you. un-take the taking of you. un-still the stillness of you

for several hours i watch a straight beam of light crossing
a closing day
it becomes appendage pointing never quivering
completely straight
in your dreams you chase dragonflies
pattern your wings from their colors

at least i want to believe that you dream because i can't un-
die you.
i can't un-die the width length breath of you. i want to un-
die the color of you the shadow fire smoke blood and water
of you.
i want to undie the sharp wet smooth ice of you. i want you
to un-die. your hair head eyes mouth teeth neck shoulders
arms elbows hands breasts belly thighs hips legs knees ribs
ankles feet of you. i want to un-die you. i want to undie
your heat your wounds your cries hugs screams whispers.
i want to un-die the house bowl cup sip swallow bite of
you. i want to un-die you. un-die the silk wool nappy
coarse sexy round and long of you. un-die your words your
songs your dance the very crawl of you

it's what a mother does. she un-dies your blood the colors
of your birth and the colors of your death. she un-dies
every crumb of you she un-dies your smell your touch your
taste she un-dies your heart. she becomes a ghost forensic
inside a tangled lullaby. you live there now in the upper
crust of my heart trespassing all the barbed wires electric
fences in its basin where you once built delicate tattered
houses fragments of leftover storms. left over childhoods.
leftover deaths.

you arrived spirit-hungry with journeying mid-wives
carolina moons and false indigo smeared across your
windows waiting to be lifted

*we are raw thrust. i wake up with the kinky salt of you
burning my mouth. blackness comes apart like corners
becoming tops becoming sides. salt burned. kinky mouth
exploding ripping off shark heads. this ocean we swim
becomes death trap. penalty to breathe. vigilante of
privilege. why is this culture of the personal so hard to
bear.*

*her tongue has forgotten the currency of okra. the
language of paw paw fruit burns like december ice under
her fingernails.*
*i have traveled to the priestess who barters for johnny
walker red. twelve gutted and cleaned drum fish. seventy-
four american dollars for the wise one in her gap-toothed
regalness.*

dusk

all the pieces of my heart slather long rays of sunlight.
dance over fruit that a heart refuses. a heart cut open into

perfect sections. one for the mother one for the father one
for the son two for the daughter. enough fruit. enough light
for the bees that gather to sting light into flowers

i've only visited your grave once before at *dusk* for i
believe it to be your quiet time. your time to visit with
granddaddy great grandmother great grandfather great
aunts great uncles cousins
in the silver air i heard you turn to listen to footsteps of a
long lost friend who trekked the skies from california
searching for your grave in the dark
dusk i find him there walking sideways with grief. holding
flowers

dusk what do you call your mornings your noondays your
evenings of moonless sky winter grace and summer frill.
what do you drink at dusk from the hands of an angel

from somewhere far beneath the hearts that love you the
memory of you dances across a threshold of stardust. your
heart sings forth a new face. how does a mother continue
to sing

how does a mother continue to whisper the story of a
daughter's death
why does the night bring me over and over again to this
river
with deaf hands a tongue learns to swim across continents
undressing mute men in holy robes holy cloth

tongues become dances inside an opera of revolution
rebellion
daughters offer open legs for the storage of gunpowder
blades bullets

while grandmothers become live spittoons for the
sharpening of hidden machetes buried deep under rotten
sugar cane
this is the march for water
this is song for the thirst of newborns dry breasts and dry
bread
the elegy of the two legged ones who come to battle
without one god in sight

who will count the children carrying alphabets of memory
beneath collapsing chins. it is this language of water that
does not translate beyond its own reflection. who will sing
the forever promises we made to each other

have mercy upon him whose capital is hope and whose
weapon is fear. we bring the soil. it is such a poetic gesture
for your journey through an ocean of sky. i've still not
named you. new star. body of my body. body of my breath.
citizen of my womb. i have been waiting for your face to
open beneath this ground and pour out seven nations.
seven generations. seven rivers. fire of my hair… crackling
like bluebirds in the farkleberries

woman-child is born to the woman-child

it is this one a.m slow dance across the floors of my mind.
disco. apartheid. harlem drive. bruised ankles of a
shackled dancer. chasing unicorns around the hudson
river. on sundays everything tastes like rain. chinese-
cuban take-out reminds me that my mouth is an un-claimed

foreign country with poppies growing along the borders. brown bag ecstasy. hartford connecticut bourgeois deception. secrets. illegal mind weapons. poems that slide off rooftops when your father's fingers foreplay the german bass violin. sundays that never promised anything beyond blue black welts hiding beneath all the colors of the artist's wand. you were born inside a room of turkish smoke. swaddled in opaque blush linen. i become the mother who has forgotten who she is. who she might me. the women chant story songs about mothers they never knew. your father's father brings white lilies. your other grandfather stretches deeper in his grave. you are born on the first anniversary of his death. he is waiting. knowing you will recognize him on the other side. she is the you. you and i become more of me. you will call on your grandfather to guide you beyond the stars. it is enough to be born in a windowless room. walls perspiring with the heaviness of rose water cinnabar rosemary. it is enough to recognize your own shadow in the middle of a hailstorm. our shadows are ghosts in a holy city. mother. daughter. forever locked inside the belly of the woman with knives.

now

i write books. store grief upside down on the top pantry shelf where seldom used wedding gifts rest beside oversized serving platters the antique tea service and those tacky fake porcelain teacups i can't bear to toss. in the books there is no grief. only food sex sultry winter music and the teeth of clowns. the genetic complexities of your death bear roots. unravel. implode.

graft themselves into continents oceans volcanoes
of blood-stained bones that will not un-die.

Hundreds of Geese Honk in Salute

Sharon Blessum

Honoring Fern Rohrer Blessum

we bury Mother
next to her only son
she who taught me
that loss needs
rituals of healing
now receives
what she gave

in a dream
I sob for my mother
'I want her back'
tears flow
as from the watering can
we used to water the graves
in childhood ritual
her with hoe
me with questions
life after death
and such

what about Roger
not baptized
I worried he could go to hell
oh he was
Dad tells me one day
in the car

as we drive away
from plots toward
my umpteenth need
to know
what happens
where is God
thus begins my lifelong study
of theology and philosophy

Today, forty years later
I plant
fifteen flowers
and my sorrow
into the ground
anger as mulch
know I'll need
a lot of digging
to have life after Mom's death

*****

The phone rings on a hot July day. It takes a long time to absorb the word *cancer*. Mom has it. In her lungs. Maybe inoperable. She is not a smoker. Everybody is in disbelief. I talk to one sister or another from seven to eleven that evening. Mom says she feels an inner strength. Wanda says Mom is aware it is hard on me to be so far away. I live two thousand miles from North Dakota.

A month later, Mom has her whole left lung removed. She is in intensive care for several days. She expresses relief that they have "caught it in time". She says she loves life and wants to take each day as it comes. I will decide whether to go out there after our commitments at Chautauqua. We had been out there just a month before her diagnosis and my vacation time is used up.

Mom is depressed after surgery. I ask if I should come. They all agree it's too far for a short visit. I am aware of some measure of relief, knowing I absorbed her depression my whole life. Yet, I want to smother her with kisses and gentle touch. Wish I lived closer.

A biopsy confirms liver cancer. Big question is whether or not to try chemotherapy. Oncologist doesn't advise it. Prognosis is a few months to live. She's 59. My sisters call often. I am indebted to them. They keep me a part of the circle. We go from unbelief to sadness, love, calm, shock. Dad is in a lot of pain.

In September, Mom tells the doctor there is one thing she wants to do—go to New Jersey to see her oldest daughter. He says, *Go.*

Mom and Dad arrived with a van full of furniture Dad made, including a black walnut headboard he'd created for their own bed. She cries, *We won't be able to use it.* I hold her. I see something in mother's eyes I have never seen before. Hopelessness, resignation, vacancy, death. She is picking out funeral hymns. She is concerned about how to divide the diamonds on her wedding ring among four daughters.

Ocean I
Mom and I go to the ocean,
eat shrimp in a basket
on a bench by the boardwalk.
  I'm not ready to leave this life.
We take off our shoes,
roll up our pants
and play at water's edge.
  It's okay if Dad remarries.
  He will always love me
  and think of me when he mows grass,
  feeds birds, weeds flowers.
We splash, foray in and out of waves.
a video saved in the gallery of my heart
  Can you help me choose a funeral bulletin?
  Which poem should we put in the service?

The night before they leave, we have a party with crab casserole. I give them a Jim Nabors tape, puzzle, seawater from our visit to Point Pleasant. In the morning, when they are ready to drive home, we stand in the driveway a long time in a long hug. Mom looks into my eyes and says *I love you. I always have.* The twelve-day visit has been deeply sad and intimately happy. I write my sisters:

Mom and Dad left this morning. I cried a long time, though we have had much happiness in their long visit here. I will always be grateful for these days. I feel guilty that I am not there to help with all that is going to unfold. And sad not to be part of all you will share together. It's hard to be so far away and it's hard to be there, too...

She needs to know her family will be okay when she is gone. I'll come when it is the right time. Help me know when that is. I love you each for your many thoughtful ways of including me in everything. I think of us holding invisible hands, and hope our bond stays strong. XO

A month later, I wish I could self-soothe as violent pains radiate across my midriff. I can find no position of comfort for over an hour. I cancel dinner plans with a friend. Later in the evening, I learn it started at the exact time mom started chemotherapy.

A week or so later, I am sitting at my writing table between 5 and 6 o'clock, I'm creating a Christmas card in honor of my mother, listening to a metaphysical tape, and thinking of Mom having her CAT scan today. Would she have chemotherapy again? Would I have stomach spasms again?

I move into meditation and invite the white light of protection. I feel calm, yet a few minutes later, I walk into the kitchen and get furious at the boys for leaving a mess. This misdirected anger turns into tears after dinner. After I cry, I sit on the steps with David and Jamie and have a good heart-to-heart. I tell them I hate being in the role of a nag, or bitch, and don't want to hurt my relationship with them. *I want to be close to you. I'd rather hire a house cleaner than scold you.* They truly listen, know they should have cleaned up their mess, and also know my reaction was overdone. When I feel the boys deserve an apology from me, they are not only attentive but also understanding.

At nine, I call Rugby. Mom and Dad have just come home. My sister Bette had put up Christmas lights on the house while they were in Grand Forks, and had Christmas music playing, and a poinsettia on the table. Sweet. Chemotherapy has not diminished the cancer but has arrested its growth. The doctor told her to eat, no more chemo for a month. I give her a pep talk—tell her we all want her around. We are her cheering section, but she is the one who has to fight. I am awake until 2 am digesting this. The next morning, I'm angry and exhausted. The ups and downs are hard on everyone.

Dream: I'm in the bathroom in my parents' home. I put up mirrors behind the mirrors. So I can see more?

In January, Mom is feeling better. I think maybe we'll drive back to the prairies in April.

I have no idea how foretelling this is.

Late in the month, they call and say they are coming here again. In fact, they'll be here this week. I go to the airport with two helium balloons, which bring smiles at the airport. They will be carried back to North Dakota to spend many weeks in their bedroom. I am excited, nervous and teary as the plane lands. I tell mom how proud I am of her making this trip; she says she has nothing to lose. I feel she is here with a purpose this time, maybe for me, because I am more able to love now. I've worked through some of my childhood issues; my heart is open to her.

When they leave, mom cries at the airport, *Take good care of Dad.* And, *I hope life will be good to you.* I thank her for these two visits, tell her how much it means to me that she has spent time getting to know my life and the boys. She tells me she is concerned that I not overwork, that I must be loving to myself, and not drained like I was in the ministry. I tell her I will not do that to myself again. *You need to love yourself first.* Though she has never done that, she means it. I assure her that I will always remember what she's just said, that if I'm tempted to work an extra hour, I'd know she wouldn't want me to. I remember this as her blessing to me. She doesn't want us to talk more. I cry when they board, harder when the plane takes off. Jamie strokes my arm.

By the first month of March, Mom has lost a lot of weight, is mostly in bed, and has pain. Dad sounds solid. He talks with me about my wish to come and spend some time with Mom when it is meaningful to her. Also, I want to be there later when she dies, though I will accept whatever happens. Henry is busy with his ministerial duties with Easter coming. My own obligations and the boys' school make planning a visit confusing.

Dream: I'm in the attic with mother. She has clothes and items labeled for us four girls. I see the two sweaters I bought in Europe and another with a picture of me on it. I realize the attic is long and narrow, like a tunnel with a light at the end. She is going on ahead. I'm okay.

Dream: my stomach hurts, tells me it wants baby food because my mommy is dying. I am to let go, the hardest lesson I experience in life. A girl's mother dies but once.

At the end of March, Mom has more pain and the medication makes her confused. There is less of her.

Then, Mom becomes incoherent but gets clear suddenly to ask for a family party that night. My father and sisters gather with her in the living room. She keeps saying to everyone, *I love you,* kissing them over and over. She wants many pictures. *It is a night that will live forever,* Dad says. They call me afterwards. Mom and I talk. She knows I am coming. I prepare to leave the next day.

On April 5th, I walk into her bedroom in late afternoon and walk around the bed to kiss her. She leaves her faraway land to actually focus on my face and offers me her beautiful, beautiful smile—her last smile. Then, just as quickly, drops back into a world we cannot reach. I thank her for waiting for me, and we confirm our love for each other.

Fresh flowers are on the bureau. Dad is playing a tape of her favorite hymns. My sisters have been here all week. They have tended her in her own bed, surrounded her with beloved objects. I am very proud of their watch with her. I hope she is seeing spirits, loved ones, whatever would lure her on in comfort. We take turns sleeping and keeping vigil with her. Everyone is kind; no one had better care. I go to bed around 11, tired from travel.

At four in the morning, I awake and go downstairs to her room. In two minutes, she turns her head and stops breathing.

*****

At Mom's funeral, the minister says that Mom knew she was a sinner, and I am furious. Of all the ways he could have begun speaking about Mom's spiritual life, he chose the oppressive, life-draining, guilt-producing identity that was so internalized by women in her generation. I want to stand and scream. *Mom knew she was loved by God.*

Instead, I close my eyes and briefly meditate:

I go inside the sun to feel its warm rays. Sunbeams touch the tears on my face, form watercolors that flow into designs. From face painting, I collect words to say how I see my mother, not as sinner but sweetheart of the hearth who labored long and hard to create family and failed only in her love of self. Jesus bows to her.

As we leave the church, a robin sings. At the cemetery, as the casket is lowered, hundreds of geese honk in salute.

Finding More Mother

Today I find more Mother
In a room I had forgotten.
I reject your culture's dismissal
of women and claim your grace
I finger lovely laces
of your tablecloths and towels,
treasures retrieved from a trunk
buried in the sea of your home.
Your elegance must be uncovered,
remnants disguised in worn apparel
can be woven to clothing and quilts
as a new rendition of you
evolving legacy
of your ancestral wisdom
to help me with the hurdles of life
I must also face
You were a lover of beauty and keepsake
my inheritance rescued from a watery womb
cherished and draped around me
as shawl of blessing
you who once seemed grey and gone
now appear in white adorned with roses
still listening to birds and opening windows
to the sun
you beloved mother
you outlive the message of death
and every piece of you I touch
is resurrection
my memory bank full
of your feather-light heirlooms
my heart lined with your love

Going Forward

Barbara Viola Ford

On Wednesday, October 28, 2014, the world my husband Paul and I knew, and took for granted, disappeared in a matter of minutes in a nondescript UNC doctor's office. The worry I'd had around his possible concussion seemed so silly now—ridiculous even.

With the words, "We're calling the ER, can you drive yourselves or do you want an ambulance?" we began a new, not-long-enough journey together.

The diagnosis was a brain tumor—the worst kind—grade VI glioblastoma. A death-sentence. 14–18 months.

Surgery, chemo, radiation. The only possible savior: a clinical trial at Duke. More heartbreak when we learned—five minutes into his first appointment—Paul wasn't a candidate. Very few people are. *A fucking brain tumor.*

The cruelest diagnosis, I thought, for a man who was so curious; and read anything and everything. A musician, a poet, a man who loved to discuss and debate. The brain tumor he had, and its position, would change all of that. It would make it hard, if not impossible, to read, to concentrate, to remember.

Oh, to remember—Paul had an incredible memory for details, song lyrics, movie lines, conversations. Now he often seemed to be on a loop track and sometimes, he knew it. This was not just a physical cancer; it was a disease that took Paul's essence. Paul—the half of us who was the extrovert, the king of small talk with substance, the man who seemingly never met a stranger—would now begin to become someone else, would begin to disappear in front of me. And me—always more the introvert. Paul's sidekick. *Where did that leave me?*

I discovered right away that traveling this journey with Paul was something we could not do on our own. It became frighteningly evident when the doctors sent us home from the hospital just two short days after brain surgery with what seemed like little or no specific instructions about what to expect. I've never, ever, been so afraid in my life. I stood in my kitchen with three friends and sobbed openly and desperately.

How do I do this? What's going to happen? I needed help and I saw it so clearly. And I knew I needed to be able to *ask* for that help. These three people standing there comforting me were waiting for me to ask, wanting to do whatever was needed. They would not be the only ones.

I'd need to step out of my comfort zone. I needed to be Paul's "front man" now. No more support role, "back office" person—as he and I jokingly called it over the years of our marriage. A role reversal was beginning to take shape. The extrovert, through no fault of his own, was going more inward. And I was being pulled out of my protective shell. It was more instinctive than conscious, more born out of necessity. But I had to, and there was no looking back.

I've never been good at asking for help. I didn't see it as a sign of weakness as much as a breach of privacy. And I was a pretty private person, especially where emotions were concerned. Paul and I shared everything and that seemed to be enough—until now. Now, I'd need to reach out beyond our protective bubble—let my guard down, be vulnerable.

Paul and I have been so fortunate to have a loving, caring, open community of people around us. Lucky for us, smart and talented people. People with skills we could use, who were not shy about offering. These local folks helped us with meals, chores, visits with Paul so I could work or run errands, bodywork and self-care, sharing music, stories, news of life outside our house.

All of this required opening our house up wide— wider than we ever had. Our little *cocoon for two* was a thing of the past.

And yet, it felt comforting. We didn't need to be alone. I learned that the people who loved me and Paul wanted nothing more than to help us somehow, some way. They needed to give as much as we needed to receive. Our community was going to be our Savior, we would simply need to let them in far more than we ever had.

As a touring musician, Paul knew people all over the US and in Canada. I "met" hundreds of these people through social media—once word got out of Paul's illness. Some of these folks had only met Paul once, for maybe fifteen minutes at a show, but felt an instant connection.

This was the consistent theme that emerged—Paul had a way of making instant, lasting connections with people he met—often only briefly. He made people feel seen and heard, like they were talking to an old friend.

Thank the universe for social media. It was instrumental in keeping us connected with folks near and far who wanted and needed to know what was going on with Paul—wanted to send him messages, well wishes, photos, remembrances. Using social media sites like Facebook and Caring Bridge helped us efficiently stay connected. And since it was me doing the communicating for both of us, it was another opportunity for me to take the lead socially, to lay myself out there and be vulnerable.

It was OK to be frank in these updates. To put it all out there—the good, the bad, the sad and disappointing, the frightening. I figured it wasn't my job to be sunny and upbeat for people. This thing sucked and everyone knew it. We were not going to pretend there might be a different outcome. If you wanted to be in the know, you needed to accept what was.

This large, caring community was mostly a gift for us. But it could also be tricky to navigate at times. People wanted time with Paul because they knew time was short, too short. There were lots of them and only two of us. There were friends from out of town, and a very large family.

The effects of the brain tumor and the treatments had gradually taken a toll on Paul's stamina and his ability to engage and communicate. Naturally, most people didn't completely see or understand that. Paul had a way of bucking himself up for company and then crashing hard afterward. Explaining this to people could be difficult and awkward—and not something I wanted to do in front of Paul either. Paul was getting more easily exhausted, confused, and overwhelmed by just a little stimulus.

Gatekeeping was not a role I relished taking on, as I generally avoid conflict and I hate disappointing people. But it was critical for whatever quality of life Paul had remaining. And if I was sure of one thing, it was that I wanted the time he had left to be the best it could be. And sometimes that was going to mean less people.

But how do I explain to people who know they may not get to see Paul ever again that he's too tired, or too weak to do a visit? And how do I make sure that he and I get enough time alone together? I needed that desperately myself. People were going to have to understand. So, another thing I discovered about myself was that I could say "no." This was a hard and fast lesson in setting boundaries.

In addition to time, I also had to set mental and emotional boundaries for myself around information—information coming from all sides. The world is sadly filled with people who have personal or peripheral experience with cancer and cancer treatments. From the first day of Paul's diagnosis, we started receiving an avalanche of advice about alternative and conventional treatments, research studies, and the like. This was another way folks just wanted to help in any way they could.

But being on the receiving end of it and needing to be the sole recipient and filter for it, was overwhelming and daunting.

All I wanted to do was keep my beloved Paul alive, so I felt like I had to try and sift through everything. *Maybe there was something out there I missed that would be the magic cure, the silver bullet for Paul.* You want to hear it all, and then you don't. You simply can't.

I received books on hydrogen peroxide treatment for cancer, mushroom therapies, electro-magnetic helmets for brain tumors. Lots of well-meaning folks out there who just want to help us. I felt like I was making excruciating choices every day, mostly by myself. Once again, I turned to my friends and family for help. I reached out with questions to them and was grateful for their counsel.

Paul did well with treatment for the first ten or so months after surgery. We were able to do a lot—spend quality time with friends and family, travel. And we realized we had never spent so much concentrated time together, just us. That was so special. I try in my grief to remember and be grateful for that time. In addition to the standard radiation and chemo treatments, Paul was lucky enough to have access to acupuncture, massage, polarity therapy, and herbal therapies. I believe all of this contributed to Paul's having a much better quality of life during these months.

But a glioblastoma has its own agenda. It will only be held at bay for so long. So, in the fall of 2016, about eleven months after Paul's initial surgery, the doctors told us the chemo had stopped working, and there weren't any other treatment options. I had to make another soul-crushing decision—ultimately by myself—but with the loving counsel of friends and family. It was time for hospice.

Paul lived for another two months. These were emotionally and physically draining days and weeks for us both. We were scared. I wanted to soak in every moment with Paul. I was so grateful for the compassionate care of the hospice team. And I needed their help to guide me with boundaries at that time more than ever. I reached out to them and also to my close friends to really be there for us.

Paul died on December 14, 2016. It was a day filled with music, stories, friends around the bed, a bonfire, a great blue heron sighting in the backyard. Everything he would love. He left us that evening at 7:30. He was ready. I knew I had to let him go, but I wasn't ready.

In the two-plus years since Paul's death I've been trying to nurture whatever extrovert is inside me, to work that muscle I developed during Paul's illness. I want to be vulnerable, open with my community of friends, be more authentic.

How do I move forward and not retreat inside again? It often feels like that's exactly what I want to do, and what would feel comfortable. But isolation and loneliness are also frightening to me. It's important for me to continue to reach out to people, connect with people, ask for help—not be afraid to be human—and reveal more of myself. This is what I was doing, what I had to do, the last fourteen months of Paul's short life. I see it as a positive that came from this tragedy and a continual learning process for me. It's also a way to try in some way to thank the people who rallied around us. To attempt to show them how grateful I am—how much I respect and love what they've done for us—by trying to be my best self, going forward.

Paul would want this for me. He would say it's time to move from the back office to the front. I want to honor him, so I'll keep working on that, hope he sees me, and is cheering me on.

My friend Chuck Tillotson died yesterday.

Gary Phillips

I dreamed of him as a bird last night,
migrating in the dark toward some vast coastal outline.
Other fliers joined as we flew.
Up ahead somewhere I could hear raucous welcome cries
and what sounded like a thousand gossiping voices.
Chuck made for it.
He shook me off somewhere
over the noisy shore with a tender but definitive dip,
and I woke up in my own body.
There were gold finches at the feeder, explosions of yellow
energy so intense that it took me long hollow seconds to
recognize them as being part of the real world.

*****

Chuck Tillotson was a carpenter, a guitar player, a legendary party boy. He laughed a lot, admired his friends and stayed true to them, gave himself freely to strangers. He was a father to beautiful boys. Chuck played a slow style of poker that drove some people crazy. He was a handsome man with a gentle mien and a long unruly white moustache. He had a voice like hot honey: low, whiskey-filtered, languorous and warm.

Chuck had a great love in his life, his wife Veronica. They had struggles, as all great loves do, but many people envied the laughter they carried together and their love gravity, the way they leaned toward each other over and again as if they shared a rich warm secret.

*****

Chuck was alive and living his life, and then he was in trouble, and then he was slipping away from us, one foot on the Long Road and no more than a slim thread connecting him to the dirt and sweat and precious air of this world.

*****

The doctor called us in for a conference, into a lounge so full of people some had to share chairs or sit on the floor. He brought in his whole nursing crew for support. The doctor was gentle, and his eyes misted, which comforted us, but his message was unequivocal. "I could do an intervention here," he said. "It's what we're trained to do as doctors. I could maybe give Chuck two or three more weeks, stem the infection with surgery and powerful drugs, but it would all come to the same thing, and I don't think Chuck would want us to do that." He blinked.

In a room just a few yards away Chuck lay, sedated and pierced with tubes. He looked so vulnerable it broke our hearts.

Veronica took her courage in hand and made the decision: Chuck would be taken off life support and his family would gather and make him as comfortable as possible. She talked with his sons and their strong fine mother, called family members, made arrangements with the nursing staff, had a final consult with the doctor.

I stood in for the family during the extubation, while the doctor and staff freed Chuck from his coil of tubes and separated him from the respirator. This procedure took over an hour. Nurses and doctors were tender and respectful, talking with Chuck as if he were conscious and making every effort not to cause him pain. They treated him always as a human being, as the treasure of a person we all knew.

At calm times during the procedure I worked with Chuck, and the staff gave me room. I blessed him with water and sang songs and prayers of release from many traditions, like this from *The Pagan Book of Living and Dying*:

Beloved Chuck, you are dying
But you are not alone.
We are here with you,
The beloved dead await you.
You go from love
into love.
Carry with you
only love.

May our love carry you
And open the way.

Lauren the floor chaplain walked up to his bed and said: "Chuck, you are a lucky man. You must be a lucky man to inspire such love, such careful attention, so many friends."

*****

After Chuck was made clean and comfortable his boys and Veronica came in and hugged him and whispered to him and held him in their arms until he died. We all cried a bucket of tears, but it was a great send-off, with 20-30 more waiting in the hall who came in after to have their time with Chuck and with the family.

That same evening Chuck's friends met at a community building on the Chatham/Alamance line and a riotous emotional wake broke out, with music, dancing and another raft of tears, floating us toward that Other Shore so close we could almost see it, but not ours, not yet.

*****

My sweet daddy died this year as well, and almost as unexpected, and I saw a conservative Baptist community I had fled taking care of its own, with food and witness and stories, and a thousand acts of kindness to our family. Both these deaths, Chuck's and my father's, were hard and shattering to me but they each had a sense of *rightness* somehow, not that they happened but that both deaths were surrounded by dignity and love and community support for the survivors.

*****

Now my father speaks through my bones in the morning dew and sometimes Chuck Tillotson will slip into my dreams. I'm glad for both, and all that went before.

Mother's Day

Amiel Landor

Miriam Anna Sperber Landor
3/6/34–5/14/17

Dear Mom,

Your death surprised me. I was not prepared for the way—or the day—you chose to go. It was Mother's Day, and I was about to cook pork chops and kale. I had a friend over, and we both realized that we needed to call our mothers. I turned off the stove and ran upstairs to give you a call at the hospital. A nurse answered, confused; she said to hold while she got the doctor. I imagined he would give me a report of your health. Instead, he asked who I was and my relation to you. Then, a long silence.

The doctor calmly stated that you had passed. My brain literally could not comprehend his words. I said in return, with agitation and insistence, "Could you please revive her so that I can wish her a Happy Mother's Day?"

I could not bridge those two realities: calling you to read a special Mary Oliver poem while being told that you had died 45 minutes prior. After the doctor told me they did everything to save you, the shock tore through my body. Every cell of my being flipped over, and then fell into free fall.

After pulling my stomach off the floor, I had enough wherewithal to speak to the nurse again. I asked her what your last moments and words were. She started to cry and said that you were beautiful. Your eyes were glistening blue. You asked to hold the nurse's hand. In true Miriam fashion, I could imagine you were comforting while being comforted, probably having found some vulnerable part of the nurse's life that you wanted to comfort *her* in. You looked straight at the nurse and told her, "Jesus is waiting for me." You glowed. She went to do her rounds and when she returned, you were gone. You did not want to keep Jesus waiting.

I wanted to hold onto the nurse myself, knowing she was the last person to ever speak with you. I wanted her to hold my hand and tell me every detail of your last moments on earth. Were you scared? Did you wish you were surrounded by your family? Or were you going to simply exit the way you came in, escorted by a wild tribe of angels, Jesus leading the pack? I went over that scene for almost a year, wishing that you had not died alone.

That is *not* how I imagined it would be. I had visions of holding your hand on your deathbed, reading poetry while soft music played in the background. As a spiritual minister and your magical youngest child, I thought I would help bridge you to the beyond. I had so much grief even considering that you could have been alone, lonely, or afraid. That is not how it was supposed to go. For me. But you and your council chose differently.

My grief finally abated when a hospice counselor told me that often several hours, perhaps days before someone dies, the veil between worlds has thinned and you are held in glorious light in what is yet to come. I want to believe that you were not alone but surrounded by light, love, and angels that you could actually see before your grand ascent. That Jesus' hand was reaching out to guide you back home.

Home. I walked back down the stairs and my friend asked how my call went. How, in the span of 10 minutes, does one's world change so dramatically? He stayed with me until 4 am. What kept crossing my mind was, "Do I still eat the kale?" Something so mundane as eating seemed sacrilegious, and yet you had never died before with a plate of kale on the table.

I went to bed, which seemed odd – like somehow I needed to stand vigil for Life itself. Who sleeps when Death has just brushed by, taking your mother with it? Upon awakening, just a few hours later, the reality of your death smacked me down again. I started crying and asked for a sign that you were alright. At that moment, I heard my wind chimes clamoring away outside in the wind. I knew it was *you*. Its tones are harmonized to Amazing Grace, one of your favorite songs. I was deeply comforted, even if for a brief moment. Now, when the wind chimes are singing away, I imagine you are reminding me of your presence: "Oh, there's Miriam, banging up a storm." When I was in Europe, you stayed on my friend's front porch, and he would occasionally send me wind chime voice messages. Beautiful!

The day after your death, I felt the most unusual sensation: my whole grounding dropped away. I hadn't realized how much your earthly presence was a part of my cellular structure. I was made from your DNA; once you lifted off, it was though my cells had to reorient themselves. There is no preparation for this. I knew how old you were, and the condition you were in at the end; however, you were the co-creator of my body and I was not prepared for the loss of you. The familiarity of you had become such an ingrained part of my existence that its absence was profound. It felt like a part of me left as well. Perhaps this is the art of grief; not *just* that you were now gone and that I will not be in earthly relationship with you, but that the breath that first gave me life vanished.

*****

"Pancakes and bacon," I said in between sobs. My friend asked how he could best serve me the morning after your death. I realized that I was hungry and wanted comforting food. As I sat on the porch on an unusually sunny day, I recounted the story of how you would comfort kids in the neighborhood by making them pancakes in the shape of the first letter of their name. I ate pancakes while laughing and sobbing simultaneously. The wind chimes kept singing on the porch.

*****

After all the calls to family, Barth kindly said that I did not have to come to Chicago to view your body; he, as your oldest son, would take care of the details. Still, every cell in me knew that I needed to see you before you were cremated. At first, I thought that I needed to see you to make it real for myself, but I would come to find out there is an innate and ancient need to bless a body before it takes a new form. I immediately flew from Vermont to Chicago, walking through the surreal haze of you being here one day and gone the next. I wanted to tell everyone I met that my mother had just died but the private desire to keep you close to my heart won out.

I got off the plane, and Barth met me. He said that we only had about an hour to get to the funeral home; that they were in the process of transitioning you for cremation. I sat on his front porch and made one of the most important calls of those past few days. I called one of my beloved friends who is a death doula. I said, "I only have about a half hour before I see my mother, and I don't even know what to do."

She calmly and ever so lovingly said, "You do know what to do. You are a healer and an ancient soul. Remember the time of old. Anoint her body with oil."

I cried and said, "but I only have an essential oil that I wear." She gently laughed and said, "Oh, your mother would love that fragrance!" I got up from the steps and told Barth that I was ready.

The funeral home stood on a busy Chicago corner, not far from one of the best lunches you and I had together. You were already in decline and your memory had greatly faded, but you emanated a sweetness that I will never forget. Your fragility made you vulnerable and receptive, far from your usual wildly active and sometimes agitated self. I told you that you could get anything from the menu, something you would say to me as a child when going to restaurants was a rare treat.

I asked you what you loved about your life and if there were memories that stood out for you. You told me stories of travel, early memories of growing up, and the gratitude for your three children. You kept looking at me with your sparkling blue eyes. I held back tears. Somewhere in my heart I knew that these conversations would end soon. I thanked you for all that you had done for me and how much I loved you. You, in turn, told me that I was one of your greatest blessings. Then, you asked for more coffee, with "lots of cream."

As I entered the funeral home, I was surprised by the formality. It certainly did *not* seem like the last place that you would be on the planet; perhaps I imagined you in your home on 61 East Fifth Avenue, or at your sister's in New Jersey, or some place that had much better art on the walls. Barth explained to the funeral director that I wanted to see my mother and 'do a small ritual with her.' I asked him if he wanted to join me, but he gently declined. He warned me that it might be really hard to see you. He had seen you right after your death.

As I walked into the room, I stopped and collected myself. An unusual calm came over me. This would be the first time I would see you dead, and the last time I would ever see you. I cannot quite describe the feeling; everything aligned in me and I knew what to do.

I reached the coffin, and said, "Hi, Mom." You did not respond. I laughed out loud and said to you, "Well, that's a first!" I felt an ease and comfort, not the fear or grossness people had warned me about. In fact, you looked beautiful. Your face was finally calm, the hardness of life swept away. Peacefulness emanated from you. I stroked your face and told you how much I loved you. I could feel your presence above me and continued to talk to you, sharing how I was going to bless your body.

My beloved friend was right—we have an ancient memory of how to ritually honor a body in the time of death. I was curious about how death had become something to fear in our culture, as if it is a stranger to life. And yet here you were, in just another 'form of life'—the death season.

I started at your head—anointing it with oil—praying to your council for your safe delivery and for your next stage in the healing process beyond. I placed my hands on each chakra of your body, clearing old energy that you did not want to take into the fire. I released from your body life's struggles, regrets, trauma, pain, and old karma. I held your feet for a long time and anointed them with oil. I found your vibrational color and ran that energetic color through your body, blessing you, healing you. As you stood above your body—watching me—I told you that you were free to go, that you were loved by many, and that you had blessed those who crossed your path. I said a prayer, sprinkled oil on your body, held your hand, and stroked your face one last time.

I put my hands on your heart. Then it was time to go. I slowly walked away from your body and said one of your favorite phrases, "Bye for now!" Gratitude and awe filled my heart. Seeing and healing you before you entered the fire will be one of the most important things I've done in my life.

*****

There is a definite before and after. For about a year, I felt disoriented, needing to find a new foundation as a woman without either parent. No matter how independent or self-sufficient I imagined myself to be, I must live now without the original breath of either one of you. True individuation at its finest.

After a year-long sabbatical traveling the world, I have come into my own in a refreshingly creative and alive way. Though I am not thanking you for your death, I am letting you know that I have made the best of it. And I often get the sense that you see me much more expansively than before. In fact, I feel closer to you in some ways.

It has been over two years since your passing. I often laugh at your choice of dying on Mother's Day. Did you think it would make your death anniversary easier to remember? I think it was part of your wild, unpredictable flair—of course Mother's Day will now always be ***your*** day. You did enjoy the spotlight, Mom!

Speaking of which, you appear almost nightly in my dreams. The dream varies, but I am acutely aware of your presence and feel like you are communicating with me.

The dreams were more pronounced in the beginning—now it feels like you are simply reminding me of your essence and that even in death, your spirit is alive. That is the takeaway: the veil between the worlds is actually very thin. We think there is this great separation, but I know from my work, my dreams, my sensitivity, and spiritual training that the Spirit world is always close at hand.

The other day, I was giving intuitive bodywork to an older female client. As she lay on the massage table, her face completely relaxed, I could not believe my eyes. She had the same mouth, nose, bone structure as you. I felt like I was staring at you. I was mesmerized. My brain could not reconcile what I was seeing with what I know, but then I got it. You were just visiting for a moment. You were letting me know that you are still nearby.

Death is not the end; it is simply another dimension. Spirit is everywhere we look, hoping to get our attention, like tendrils of the Divine reaching through to the earth plane, massaging our limited brains and saying "Look, look, we are here!" The beauty is that *now* I see you in an expansive, full way; you are not limited by the struggles of your body and mind. Our relationship has transformed—now it is multidimensional—full of love, grace, and singing wind chimes. Thank you, Mom.

Bye for now ~

Much love,

Amiel

On Finding One's Way

Edwin Nothnagel

It was a sunny morning, February 21, 2007. I was working at my desk in my home in Chatham County, North Carolina when I received a phone call. The line was silent for several seconds.

My stepmother spoke with a shaky and emotional voice, "Ed, your father has committed suicide."

I felt the bottom drop out of my being.

I cried and howled with pain. When the intensity subsided enough for me to speak, I asked what had happened. My stepmother said she and my father had not been getting along lately, and that they had a big fight earlier that morning. When she left for work, my father told her that he wouldn't be there when she got home.

My stepmother called my father several times with no answer and began to worry. She returned home to find his car in the driveway—his keys and wallet in the house. She called the sheriff. He arrived shortly at their home in the suburbs of Atlanta.

The sheriff was searching their house and grounds when he noticed the sound of a lawnmower running in the shed. He opened the door and discovered my father's body slumped in the seat of his riding lawnmower with a half smoked Camel cigarette in his lap.

The sheriff came into the house and reported what he had found, saying that it was a pretty smart and painless way for my father to kill himself.

I was numb and disconnected. I asked my stepmother how she was faring. She was devastated and distraught. Had she called my sister? She had.

Four days later, I am sitting in the front row of a church in south Atlanta attending my father's funeral—surrounded by my immediate and extended family. A preacher with a full head of carefully coiffed hair, a powder blue polyester suit, and matching white belt and shoes, is talking in front of the funeral crowd.

It's obvious that this man did not know my father and did not take the time to learn who he was. He glosses over the facts about my father and then gets down to some serious preaching. "Who wants to be saved?" Save me from this spectacle that has nothing to do with my father.

*****

Flash back to 1955. I was born on August 1st at approximately 6:30am, at Piedmont Hospital in Atlanta, Georgia. After a long, heavily drug-induced labor—I was given my father's name with the suffix "III" attached to the end of it. Growing up, I was told by family and friends that I was just like my father. I always wondered what people meant. He was quiet and detached from the family when he was at home. I did not know him.

Occasionally, I would see my father interact with his work colleagues. He was verbose and full of expression with these men. I would study him as he talked with his friends and wonder, "Who is this man? Why is he never like this at home?"

It became my goal to find out who he really was. I started asking for his advice or help. He was always willing to help but would never open-up and talk with me like he did with his colleagues. I was frustrated, hurt, confused, and no closer to knowing my father. I took his emotional unavailability to mean that I didn't belong.

*****

Flash forward to May 2007. I'm still in grief. My sleep is disturbed. I wake in the middle of the night and feel a presence. The hairs on the back of my neck stand up. I can't explain why, but I know this presence is my father. Every night, I am awakened by him.

I mention this to my office mate, and he offers a way forward. His wife is Lakota Sioux and they conduct regular sweat lodge ceremonies to heal, to seek wisdom, and to purify the mind, body, and soul. I needed some of that and gratefully accepted.

The sweat lodge was held near my home, and I was excited to experience this sacred ritual in hopes of finding peace for myself and my father. I entered the low, domed lodge wearing only a towel around my torso. My colleague was responsible for heating the stones on a fire outside and transporting them into a pit in the center of the lodge, while his wife conducted the ceremony.

The heated stones were placed, and the door flap was closed. It was dark, hot, stuffy, and steamy. She spoke ancient and sacred words and then stopped speaking altogether. When she started again, it was in a strange voice not at all like her own. The strange voice said that it was my father. He was sorry for killing himself and for not being there for me. He said that he was stuck between worlds.

When our ceremony was complete, my colleague and his wife said they did what they could do to help my father pass over and find peace. I was stunned and angry.

And I still did not know who he was.

*****

A few years ago, my wife attended a weekend workshop that empowers people through distinctions in language, and when she returned home, she was different in a good way. I couldn't put my finger on what the difference was. She requested that I attend the workshop. I was skeptical and resisted for a while, but I trust her judgement and eventually agreed to attend.

It was life-changing for me.

I went with the intention of finding out why my clients were not rebooking, and what I got was compassion for myself for the first time in my life. With that compassion,

I forgave for father. Forgave him for not being there for me as a child. For killing himself.

This compassion was short lived. I found myself angry at him again and started to feel his presence in the middle of the night once more. I had no peace of mind around my father, and I felt that he did not have peace either.

I had heard about a presentation by a local woman about shamanism, a spiritual practice from indigenous cultures that involves reaching altered states of consciousness in order to perceive and interact with the spirit world. I was fascinated and scheduled a session with her.

I entered the shaman's office with anxiety, but she put me at ease. The whole experience was magical, full of out-of-the-ordinary sounds, smells and sensations. In her journey, she found a malevolent entity stuck to my solar plexus—one that feeds on fear and anger. This entity had been passed down along my paternal lineage going back countless generations. The shaman was able to capture it and release this spirit to the universe.

I felt that she was able to help my father pass over and I knew he had peace at last. I felt light, spacious, grateful and exhausted. The cycle had been broken.

*****

Six years have passed, and I still struggle to find my way in life. My feeling of not belonging and not being heard has taken its toll on me, my marriage, and all my other relationships. But my experience with my father's death made me aware of a pattern: I have lived my life through the fractured lens of my relationship with my father.

Before his death, I had been following his path; it was like being on an unconscious treadmill of doing what my father did. He divorced my mother 20 years ago and committed suicide 12 years ago. It took his death to realize that I had been treading that path also.

Now I am on an exploration to discover who I am rather than who he was.

The Parable of the Mustard Seed

Mike Wiley

"Oh comfort me, dear brother, won't you tell me what you know? For somewhere in this painful world is a place where I can go." —Peter Ham

The call came just after supper on a warm Spring afternoon in April of 2017. I'm not sure why I answered it—the number was unfamiliar to me. That time of day is reserved for my family to unwind and prepare for bedtime rituals, and I rarely answer a call from an unknown number. But in between ushering my littlest one into the shower, and awkwardly folding laundry, I answered it.

Folding laundry is a skill I've never been particularly adept at—even though my brothers and I folded, sorted and washed our own clothes as soon as we could walk it seems. We washed dishes, vacuumed, made our own breakfasts, foraged for our own lunch, and followed hastily scribbled dinner instructions that ranged from "thaw and microwave" to "thaw and fry." My mother worked the "third shift" as it's called in the blue-collar world. Eleven at night 'til seven in the morning. This meant we were alone often, and even when she was home, she was asleep a fair amount of the time. She was young and single, with a *sometime* boyfriend who had a *sometime* temper.

I was the middle son in a family of three boys. The oldest, Tyrone, had a four-and-a-half-year head start on me. I call him Ty, but everyone outside the family calls him—John. The youngest, Dee, was nine and a half years behind me. Ty and I had come through the fire together; spankings, strict curfews, living in the projects. While Dee seemed to waltz through the world unscathed as the youngest of any brood may tend to do. Watching the home front battles from the safe confines of toddlerhood, unaware of any concluding conflict.

"Michael?" the voice at the other end of the line asked. It was my older brother's girlfriend Sue. She didn't have an urgency to her voice, but she never did. She also never called. They'd been together on and off for a number of years, and she had never called me in all that time. This was the only clue I had that something was in fact, wrong.

"John collapsed in Home Depot. He just fell out, saying something like, 'Gimme a second.'" Because he'd had diabetic episodes before, alarm bells weren't quite going off just yet for me, perhaps not even for her. Ty was the talker and the jokester of our family, and even a number of surrogate families he'd endeared himself to over his lifetime. I'm sure she didn't imagine, "Gimme a second," would be the last words she'd hear him utter.

Sue needed me to come to Charlotte where they lived, where he was now hospitalized. Even though they'd lived together for years, she couldn't sign paperwork or make decisions for him if he was unable to do so himself. The fact that she had called to tell me heightened the situation. He'd been in and out of the hospital with fluid around his heart or legs a handful of times in the last three years. More than once, I had no idea he'd been hospitalized until after he'd been released.

Unfortunately, this way of "living" is a cultural norm in the black community. Loved ones of a certain age were in and out of the hospital because they'd let their "sugar" or "salt"—as diabetes, and high blood pressure are colloquially called, get a little too high. Granted, Ty was on the young side. He was none-the-less keeping the cultural tradition alive by shuffling from doctor to doctor, clinic to clinic, and ER bed to ER bed—being poked, and prodded, and even having parts of his foot amputated due to his inability or perhaps stubbornness to control his "sugar." He was living his middle age years in the same way our late grandfather, his namesake, Daddy John had lived them—slowly being consumed and controlled by controllable diseases linked directly to *what* he consumed.

"I need you to come sign paperwork," Sue said, "I don't think they'll let me, and he won't wake up." Then it hit me. Ty was not conscious, and he hadn't been since he "fell over" in the Home Depot. This was a different medical situation than any that had come before it. He'd always been able to tell the paramedic or nurse what had happened and how he felt at the time. Sue clearly knew this time was different.

"I'm on my way. Text me the name of the hospital," I said, throwing toiletries in a bag and the "cloak of maturity," on my back. This wasn't an actual item of clothing but a mindset I'd grown accustomed to shifting to—or grinding toward like a rusty fifth gear—when all eyes looked upon me for answers. Tough decisions, money loans, and life advice all tend to fall on the eldest in a family. Although I was the middle child, they were shoved at me. Tossed to me. And sometimes left hanging mid-air waiting for someone—me—to pick them up. When I told my wife what happened, and where I needed to go, she understood, because she was used to it as well. I kissed the family goodbye and started the long worrisome drive to Charlotte.

Ty was placed in a part of ICU reserved for patients being kept alive on life support systems. That's what I was told by his attending nurse moments after I walked into his room. His chest and belly rose up from the bed, distended with the awkwardly taut sheets tucked over him. His face was puffy and ashen. A breathing apparatus extended out of his mouth and his nostrils looked like if he felt it, it would probably irritate his newly shorn goatee.

Ty was always extremely conscious of his looks, from his shoes to his hair. In the black community, if you could brush your hair into a tight pattern of waves using a durag, a can of pomade and patience, you deserved and received the highest respect from your peers—regardless of the latest popular hairstyle. Ty had tight waves in his early teens when most guys his age were struggling to keep a "fresh cut" or rather a nicely measured hairline. And when high top fades became popular in the eighties, his had to be the highest. His patent leather shoes had to be the shiniest. The white trim around his shell-toe Adidas had to be the whitest, and his goose feather bomber jacket had to be the fluffiest. He was every bit an 80s B-boy, and I looked up to all of it. He popped and locked and beat boxed. He wore Kangols and track suits, rayon and airbrushed blue jeans.

To me, he *was* style, and I could never pull it off, and therefore, rarely attempted to. He wore eighties hip hop culture like a second skin, while any attempt I made at doing the same seemed false—a facade—a nerd in style hound's clothing.

"His heart stopped when he initially collapsed. EMS was able to revive him, but not before the lack of oxygen to his brain had a catastrophic effect," the attending nurse carefully explained to Sue and me. "We are basically in a wait-and-see situation," she continued. "Wait to see if there is brain activity in the next twenty-four hours."

We nodded stoically, Sue and I, while the nurse told us as much as it seemed she could. When she finally paused, the silence seemed cavernous—like a great mortal vacuum that could not be filled, though we tried. We asked questions that we didn't want to know the answers to. We needed to hear some glimmer of hope in her voice. "After twenty-four hours if there is no brain activity..." She trailed off assuming we knew the rest. She assumed correct.

She turned to Sue, "Are you the wife?" Sue hesitated and I blurted out "yes she is." I was prodded by the cloak of maturity, knowing if she said "no," she could be left out of critical decisions she had every right to be a part of. Literally life and *death* decisions.

I'd seen this up close before in reverse. My mother's longtime boyfriend Gentle Lee—yes, his first name was Gentle—lay dying in intensive care. My mother who had been by his side through sickness and in health for nearly twenty years, was relegated to the sidelines while Lee's siblings made decisions she should have had a hand in.

I remembered that late night when Lee passed away. My mother and I sat by his side in the dark. She had fallen asleep and just as she dozed off—probably for the first time in days—he died. I whispered to him, "Peaceful journeys Lee. You were a good man. Truly the best, truly gentle." I lightly nudged my mother awake. She sighed deeply and caressed him. Whispered something unintelligible into his ear and pulled herself up from the bed in herculean manner. It was a level of strength I was sure I could never achieve.

As we drove into the night under a bright full moon, I asked her if she wanted me to take her home. She hesitated a moment or two, staring out of the window at the starry sky. In a voice barely above a whisper, she recounted, "When your uncle Johnny died, his wife Grace called Mama from Seattle, in the middle of the night. She told her Johnny had suffered a heart attack and passed. Mama was devastated." Johnny was my mother's oldest brother, a career Air Force officer, and my grandmother's pride and joy.

"Mama called my sister," she lamented, "and expected her to come over and comfort her. But she didn't. She was all alone." This clearly had been weighing on her for some time. I took the cue and guided us to my grandmother's home. As we walked in, my grandmother embraced her as my mother silently sobbed on her shoulder.

I couldn't watch that happen again. Legally, my mother would have to sign certain paperwork for Ty. But Sue would not be a signatory afterthought, if I could help it.

"Will one of you be staying the night?" the nurse asked.

I could see that Sue was spent, and again I was shoved by that cloak, "I am."

Sue let out the breath she'd been holding, "Thank you Michael, I just..."

"It's fine," I said, attempting to soothe any guilt she felt bubbling. "You've been through enough."

She had. It was now close to midnight and her sister had come to drive her home. I'd never met her before, but she looked at me and said, "You must be Michael. John talks about you all the time." Her words came as a shock to me. Ty and I had only recently begun to reconnect.

We had baggage as any brothers of vastly different interests and personalities might. I went to college while he went into the Army. I went to graduate school when he went into prison. We had divergent paths and a growing resentment that all came to a head in the summer of 2005, my wedding. He asked to sing a song. He had a lovely voice and with direction could have gone miles further as vocalist than I ever have as an actor. He came to the rehearsal dinner and the festivities that followed that evening. The next day as everyone arrived at the wedding, he could not be found. My mother and my grandmother requested that we delay the ceremony in hopes that he'd appear. He never did, nor did he ever have an answer for not doing so.

It broke my heart, and we didn't speak for several years. When we finally did, our conversations were wooden and short. It was several years until we could truly be ourselves around one another. One night during a dinner stop I made between performances in Charlotte, I asked him why he skipped out on my wedding. He blew it off in the way he blew off serious things, with a Sammy Davis Jr. "I gotta be me," smile. Granted, I had asked the question in the way I typically asked him serious questions, with a flippant, "Just out of curiosity," chuckle. It's the way I'd come to talk to him. He found me too cerebral, and I found him too glib.

Shortly after Sue and her sister left, the attending nurse returned again to check Ty's vital signs. She paused in her bedside routine, "Talking to him could help. I've seen it happen. If he just hears your voice, it could stir something."

I nodded and said, "Thanks."

As I stared at him in the dim light of the small room, I began to speak. It came out in a trickle at first, in the way I had talked to him at times when he was conscious— jokingly so he wouldn't think me too cerebral. But as the night wore on, my facade began to drop, speaking honestly about our lives together, and the men we had become. I cursed him for not taking care of his body—his disease—knowing that what I was really cursing was the time I'd lost being angry at him, and not finding a pathway to one another's heart.

And when I could curse no longer, I pleaded with him to come back.

To come back for his daughter. To come back for his brothers. To come back for my mother and Sue. And when I ran out of loved ones, I rattled off things he loved, like the Pittsburgh Steelers and UNC Basketball, shiny rims and movies he laughed out loud to. Finally, memories. "Come back for the memories we share, man," I begged. Those memories poured from me in those early morning hours alone in his hospital room.

In 1997, Ty was working security at a club near downtown Charleston, West Virginia. I happened to be passing through with a small theater company for one night. We were staying on the outskirts of town. He offered to come pick up me and a couple of folks I was working with and take us down to a club he was a bouncer at. So, Ty and his long time, best friend Cedric rolled up to the hotel at about ten or eleven o'clock at night, ready to go. I can't remember what kind of car they pulled up in but let's just say—for the sake of the story—that it was a lime green Lincoln Town Car. Because Ty always liked big cars with booming systems and tight shiny rims. Because he himself boomed through life boisterous and unapologetic. And like those classic, early model American cars that we as kids longed to drive, or ride in, or get a good view of before they passed—Ty was leaving us too soon.

Some of my earliest memories of my big brother took place in big cars. In the seventies, long before there were car seats and mandatory seatbelt laws, we sat in the back of my mother's Gran Torino. We cruised down small city blocks. Me on the left side of the car and Ty on the right side. We'd lay our heads back watching out the back rectangular window and count the streetlights as we rode home listening to AM WTOY. Tyrone singing along to the Isley Brothers... "drifting on a memory... "or The Bee Gees... "And where are you now, now that I need you." or The O'Jays..." She used to be my girrrrrl..."

That night in Charleston cruising toward his club was no different; Ty crooning old school classics as we sped down Interstate 64. The four of us, my co-workers and I in the back; the two of them, Ty and Cedrick in the front. Gliding towards downtown Charleston—drifting on a memory through the West Virginia mountains—laughing and lifted. Until that early model Lincoln Town Car with the silver rims stalled.

The engine quit running a mile from our destination in the middle of highway. The backseat quietly panicked while the front seat remained calm and collected. The car continued to literally drift, as if we were being carried or pushed.

As we rolled along at thirty five miles an hour, Ty pointed out that the club was down the offramp, through the center of town, a right turn, another right turn and "all we got to do is make it," Ty said without care or worry. To which his friend Cedrick co-signed with a "yup." I silently apologized to my friends because I *straight up thought* the rest of the night was going to be spent on the side of the road or walking back to the Travel Lodge. I should have had more faith. Because Ty was right. *All we had to do was make it.*

And we proceeded to coast down the offramp, through the center of town, a right turn, another right turn and we pulled right up in front of the club. Ty looked back at us and said, "Ya'll good?" That was the most proud I'd ever been to call him brother. It was just so perfectly Ty. Smooth. Effortless.

Now, here in his hospital room, I just wanted him to "gimme a second."

*****

As dawn crept into the room and he lay still silent, I wiped away my tears and called my mother. It was the hardest call I'd ever made.

There is an ancient story called The Parable of The Mustard Seed. Kisa Gotami's only son had died. In her inconsolable grief she asked the Buddha to bring him back. He said he would. The price to revive her son was simple: a handful of mustard seed. However, the mustard seed had to come from houses where the inhabitants had suffered no loss; had never grieved a loved one's death.

So Gotami began her search, journeying from house to house asking, "Did a son or daughter, a father or mother, die in your family?" They answered her, "Alas! the living are few, but the dead are many. Do not remind us of our deepest grief." There was no house where some beloved one had not died.

Kisa Gotami finally thought to herself, "How selfish am I in my grief! Death is common to all; yet in this valley of desolation there is a path that leads him to immortality who has surrendered all selfishness." The Buddha replied, "He who seeks peace should lose the arrow of lamentation, and complaint, and grief. He who has loosed the arrow and has become composed will obtain peace of mind; he who has overcome all sorrow will become free from sorrow and be blessed."

*****

Dusk had begun to settle on the second evening of Ty's hospitalization. My mother arrived, driven by my younger brother and accompanied by Ty's daughter. At this point, the attending nurse had already more-than-hinted to Sue and me that the chances of Ty surviving without life support was miniscule. He was, by all medical diagnoses, brain dead.

My mother—being deeply religious—prayed over him, caressed his hands, and whispered to him. His daughter was bereft with grief, laying her body on his and begging him to wake up. "Wake up Daddy, please!" she wailed.

He did not, and he would not, the attending nurse finally had to inform us. My niece was now inconsolable, so much so that she had to be practically dragged from the hospital room. Once again, my mother's strength astounded me. Yes, she wept and prayed, but like Kisa Gotami she steadied herself with an air of peace, and "loosed the arrow of lamentation and complaint".

Then one by one, each of us stepped into the still dimly lit room to say our last goodbyes. Myself, Sue, my mother, and Ty's daughter found corners of the ICU floor to grieve privately while we awaited our turn at his bedside. Then, the nurse simply whispered, "Mr. Wiley" in a way that assured me we could have all the time we needed. I relayed that assurance to the family. We took our cues from Sue, who was ready to let the love of her life start his long walk home.

As the machines keeping his heart pumping went silent, our tears fell, and we stepped out of the room for the final time. We held one another in our grief, in our memories of our big brother, my mother's son, my niece's father, and Sue's partner. We weren't yet in that place of peace The Buddha had advised. But peace was present, off in the distance and as Ty would have predicted, "All we had to do was make it."

Beautiful Little Bird

Diane Fine

I am the youngest of three girls. Beth, Janet and me. Three sisters who—consciously or not—existed in relation to each other. My mother was very organized and liked to plan. There are two years between each of us, her daughters. Later in our lives, she told me that the time when we were all under ten years old was the most precious years of her adulthood. I like to picture her with her three little ducklings—tumbling around and over each other—establishing our respective places in this family that was physically very orderly and emotionally quite chaotic.

Our parents were part of the "greatest generation." My father served in WWII. They met on a blind date after the war, married, and raised us in a small G.I. house on Long Island in a suburb of New York City. I felt a solid foundation of love and support, but my mother was tired, more mellow, less involved with my day-to-day doings than she had been with Beth and Janet.

I clearly remember my mother sitting me down one day when I was about ten or eleven. She said that she had attended all the open-school nights, band events, and chorus concerts for my sisters. Would I mind very much if she passed on most of those events for me? I was a good student and citizen and she felt I would not be particularly affected one way or another by her presence. My father's presence was never expected as he worked very long hours six days a week.

Looking back, it seems I could have felt disappointed by this request, but I only remember understanding her point of view. This was the 1970s and many of my friends had stay-at-home moms. I was proud of the fact that she worked outside of the home, and, that we had the kind of relationship that enabled her to broach such a subject with me.

My oldest sister Beth—by her nature more than by circumstance—began to take on some of my emotional and logistical caregiving. She was one of the smartest, most adventurous, life-loving, and generous people I would ever know. Beth and my mother were both a ground note for me; but unlike my mother, the terrain of Beth and my relationship was neither rocky nor prone to storms.

As a young teenager, I became interested in art. Beth excitedly accompanied me on that journey by taking time from her busy college schedule to ride the train into New York City where we visited art galleries. Our favorite was the Museum of Modern Art. I have a very clear memory of Beth announcing during a semester break that she had signed up for a contemporary art history course so that she would learn more about what I loved.

We even attended one of the first presentations of Judy Chicago's Dinner Party in 1979 at the Brooklyn Museum, marrying our budding feminism with our love of art. We wandered through the anterooms leading up to the exhibit, which displayed a bounty of information about women's accomplishments throughout history. We absorbed the new material with pride and later brooded about the ways in which our foremothers had been written out of history.

Years later, when I was in college and Beth was living and working as a Genetic Counselor in Omaha, she scraped together the money for my airfare so that I could come and spend Thanksgiving with her in the Midwest. Years later, reading through letters that she had sent me when I was in college, I was astonished to see that she had written to me once a week for those four years. I came upon the flurry of correspondence leading up to that Thanksgiving visit.

Each letter ended with a countdown...

Seven more weeks until you get here.

Six more weeks until you're here.

Beth was a sister among sisters.

*****

When I was sixteen, Nana Gertie had a heart attack and was hospitalized. By then my sisters were away at college. A few days into her hospital stay, my father took me aside and told me that she was going to die. I remember not being able to comprehend what he was saying because I somehow believed that if a person made it to the hospital "on time," they wouldn't die.

One evening during the ten days or so that she was dying, my father brought me to see Nana in the hospital. I hadn't been visiting her because she was in the Intensive

Care Unit and "hooked up" to lots of tubes and wires. When we emerged from the elevator on her floor, we walked silently to her bedside. Nana was in a deep sleep. My dad, usually a gentle and jovial person, raised his voice to rouse her and called, "Mama! Mama!!"

He pushed me forward in front of him, his hands on my upper arms, saying "Mama! Look who's here! Look who's here! Do you know who this is?! Do you see who's here?!" I was terrified that she wouldn't know me. I pushed back against my dad because I wanted to leave her bedside. But he held me there and kept calling to her. I was shocked and angry and then, her eyes fluttered and opened. She looked at me, smiled and said weakly, "It's my sheyn feygele!" Beautiful little bird. Her loving spirit was still with her, and I was able to say goodbye. Later I thought about the fact that she hadn't called me by my name but by the Yiddish nickname she used for all of her grandchildren. It made sense. I was the representative for our generation. When she saw me, she saw all of us.

*****

Our mother died suddenly at the age of sixty-five in the winter of 1993. She had been hospitalized with flu-like symptoms on a Thursday. Beth was living in Chicago, Janet in Boston, and I in upstate New York. Our father called when she was admitted to the hospital. He told us that there was no need to come home. The doctors were being extra cautious.

We—my mother's three daughters—became worried about her. We agreed that our father's ability to communicate with us about the situation and interface with the doctor was not his strong suit. Janet volunteered to fly there and contact us as soon as she arrived.

Janet's phone call was a shock. "Mommy's dying. Her kidneys have failed. I'm going to go in and see her in a minute and I will tell her you are on your way." I hung up, walked to my kitchen sink, and started to retch. I felt myself falling through a deep tunnel. Was it a well? I travelled through this passage, feeling immersed in water. And then, suddenly, I kicked off the bottom and shot back up into my kitchen—back into my life.

I called a dear friend who headed over to be with me. It was snowing heavily. I had to get a flight, pack my bags, and quiet the questions and fears flooding my mind enough to get to my mother, my family.

Thirty minutes later, Janet called back. My mother had died, and she had not gotten to see her. The doctors and hospital staff never let her into the ICU. When Janet and my father arrived, the doctors were working to "bring her blood pressure back up."

Janet asked if my mother could speak to them and the doctor said, "No."

Then she asked if my mother could hear her if she spoke to her and the doctor said, "No."

He excused himself to go back in and continue the effort of raising her blood pressure. Moments later, the doctor came out to tell my sister and my father that my mother had died. They did get to go in and be with her still-warm body.

I am sure that the doctors did what they could to keep my mother in this life. But I have found what the doctor told my sister, a source of pain and outrage. He said that our mother would not be able to hear her if she spoke to her. There is no way that he could have known that. I will never understand why he didn't just say, "I don't know."

*****

A year later, a few months before her thirty-eighth birthday, Beth called to tell me she had just been diagnosed with breast cancer. The fear of losing her filled me completely and immediately. I couldn't imagine living without her. I was crying when we hung up.

Moments later she called back to comfort me.

"What are you afraid of?"

She asked me that question over and over again.

"What else are you afraid of? What else?"

As I answered her, she addressed my fears one by one.

I went to Chicago and joined other loved ones in the waiting room during her surgery. I stayed a few days and was there when she got the news. Her lymph nodes were involved, and the tumor was larger than they had originally thought.

When I got home, I was furious. I called the Rabbi of my synagogue and ranted to her.

"I will not go to another funeral! I refuse!"

Of the words of comfort she then shared, I remember this advice, "Do not bury your sister while she is very much alive."

Beth had access to excellent healthcare and endured seriously invasive treatments with strength and optimism. She was thirty-seven when she felt the lump in her breast and her beloved sons, Joshua and Aaron, were seven and four. She was devoted to them and managed to be present for them despite the hardships of her illness. When going through her first round of chemotherapy that resulted in hair loss, she wore a wig when the kids were around and when she was "out in the world." It was hot and uncomfortable, so when at home alone she often went without it.

One day she saw the boys off to school—and had just taken off the wig—when Aaron burst back into the house. Seeing her bald head for the first time, he blinked, didn't miss a beat and blurted out, "Bad hair day mom!"

Initially, Beth had conventional chemotherapy treatment. When it became clear that the cancer had metastasized, she began a more experimental protocol. Beth had at least two years of reprieve from the worst of the disease, during which she kept on, steadfast, moving forward. In a letter to her oncologist she wrote, "[I am finding] a balance between bemoaning my fate, envisioning my final days and laughing about the fact that nothing else can really be so terrible."

On one visit, I overlapped with Beth's dear friend Diane who was visiting from out-of-town. Beth was recovering from surgery, performed to shore up her hip, which had become compromised by the cancer in her bones. Beth was just starting to get around but had not yet left the house for any length of time. She told Diane and me that she wanted to attend the Purim carnival at her synagogue. Her son Aaron would be operating a booth where participants tried to knock down some stacked cans or bowling pins for a prize. Aaron was excited to be in charge and to hawk his game as part of a fundraiser for the Jewish community.

We carefully helped Beth into the car and drove down to the Temple. She was using a cane and was a bit unsteady. When we entered the social hall, she was immediately surrounded by well-wishers who had not seen her in a while. We managed to get her over to Aaron's booth where he smiled, waved, and kept up the pace that the responsibility demanded. Beth laughed and kvelled to see him, so earnest and adept.

In a short while, Diane prompted me to help her get Beth home. She felt she was being overwhelmed by the crowd and, true to character, she was not going to pull herself away unless we did it for her. Diane went to get the car, and I steered Beth through the crowd to the lobby.

When we arrived back at her house, no one else was home, and the three of us sat down in the living room and quietly wept. We each knew why we were crying though we had not given voice to what appeared to be the truth about Beth's condition. After a few moments, Beth said "I'm not afraid to die, I just don't want to miss everything."

For the entire four years of Beth's illness, I lived with my heart in my throat. I was desperately afraid she would die. I was hungry to have time with her, as if I could store her up. I was jealous of the time she spent with others. I often wanted her all to myself, as had been my privilege and pleasure so often in our childhood. I could not believe that God—in whom I may or may not believe—had chosen Beth. Why devastate three sisters that were such a profound trio?

As I grieved, I listened to Nina Simone sing her version of the great spiritual Sinnerman. I called out the words over and over, lingering on these most weighty and most demanding:

"[Lord] Don't you see me prayin'?!
Don't you see me down here prayin'?!"

On May 7, 1998, Janet called to tell me that Beth needed us to donate platelets. She was rejecting the ones from the blood bank. Because we're sisters, she would be more likely to accept them from us. The next day, I called Beth in the hospital to tell her I'd made the necessary arrangements with the Red Cross.

"Deanie, I have something to tell you. I'm dying and it's going to be soon."

"I know," I said. "I love you."

My sister Janet, her fiancé Larry, our father, my dear friend David, and I flew out to Chicago when Beth's trusted oncologist—as he had promised he would—told her that there was nothing else to be done to extend her life. Janet and Larry were scheduled to be married in October, and Beth had taken great pleasure in helping with the planning.

The day before we flew out, Beth called Janet and said, "I know now that I won't be here for your wedding."

Janet asked, "Will your Rabbi marry us in your living room tomorrow?"

Beth was overwhelmed with joy and gratitude.

Janet simply said, "Remember? I told you I wouldn't get married without you there."

By Saturday evening, friends and family started arriving from all over the country to say good-bye—and to their surprise and pleasure, to attend Janet and Larry's wedding. Beth's friends borrowed a dress for Janet and got flowers and a cake. Her Rabbi blessed Janet and Larry. He then called on all of us in the room to say our good-byes to Beth and reminded us that her light would never go out.

The following night, Beth slipped into a very deep sleep. She could no longer make it to her bed, so she slept on the couch in the living room. Janet and I sat with her throughout the night. We sang to her. We talked to each other. We helped her when she seemed uncomfortable. At 5:00 a.m. I remember lying down on the couch in the basement and waking an hour later in a complete panic that maybe Beth had left, and I hadn't said a final good-bye.

But she was still there. Not conscious. Asleep? There. Her husband had made the decision to have her moved to the hospice floor of Northwestern Medical Center in downtown Chicago, the same hospital at which she had given birth to her sons. Janet and I agreed with that decision. We had no idea how long she would be there, how long it would take for her to transition from this world to the next.

Two days. She never came back to consciousness, but she was peaceful and surrounded by friends and family. Janet, Beth's husband, her son Josh and I slept in the room with her that night. It was close quarters, silent except for the sound of Beth's breathing: deep, loud, sometimes out of rhythm. I remember lying on my cot, staring into the darkness, and trying to match my breathing to hers.

Beth died the following evening at around 9:00 p.m. I had asked the hospice nurses a few questions in the time that we were there, all of them could be reduced to, "How will we know when she is about to die?" They had shared their experiences and talked about urine output and the color of her extremities. But they also said, "You will know." They were right.

Suddenly, all of us in the room heard her breathing change. We approached and made a circle around her bed. Her husband held one of her hands. On the other side of the bed, Janet and I sat together on an upholstered footstool. I held Janet around her waist, and she held Beth's other hand. We were all silent.

Beth's breathing would stop for a while and then begin again. Then she took in what was to be her last breath and her eyes slowly opened. This surprised us and spontaneously invited us to break our silence. We all said our goodbyes in a soft, uplifting chorus. I saw the spark of life leave her body. It was exquisitely beautiful. She was no longer in her body clothes. She was no longer in pain. She was no longer in the space between life and death. She was going to be forty-one forever. I remember thinking with extreme clarity, "This is what a birth must be like, miraculous."

I left her bedside to call my father and tell him that his oldest child had just died.

*****

In the first year after Beth died, I designed and hand-printed a book entitled *Beautiful Little Bird: I Can Hear Your Song*.

Three years ago, Aviva Beth was born. Beth's granddaughter is a special light in the lives of our entire family. Aviva means "spring" in Hebrew. New beginnings, new life. We call her Avi, which, in a specific Latin form means "bird." Another sheyn feygele. Beth's sheyn feygele.

Courting Death's Atmosphere

Angela Belcher Epps

My breath ran hard and tight that season of tending to my dying Aunt Dot. Five days a week, I drove from Staten Island to the Bronx. Made a detour through Jersey to drop off my three-year old to play with my best friend's kids. I listened to the radio while I drove, but I cannot remember one song that accompanied me along those highways.

I traveled close to a hundred miles each day to keep the atmosphere of death from taking over Dot's home. Her husband was stunned stupid, and their son was twenty-two and ill prepared for the crisis of a mother dying before his eyes. I, on the other hand, had dealt with death and its issues all my life.

I remembered the months of sickness leading to my grandmother's death when I was nine years old. I was living with my grandparents, and down-slipping episodes changed our lives one week at a time. Grandma's moans filtered into my dreams as I lay in the small room across the hall from theirs. Her rural woman's agenda: starting fires, pumping water, toting wood, making biscuits, cooking on a woodstove, gave way to visits to the doctor and long periods of rest in a kitchen chair. Then there came some summer weeks when Grandpa, Uncle Bob, and I ate confusing dinners without taste or comfort as we waited for my grandmother's return from the hospital in Chapel Hill.

Mercifully, my mother appeared—taking leave from her job in Brooklyn to run the household during Grandma's extended hospital stay. Mom's presence removed the cloud of gloom that had hovered. She brought hot meals back to the table and conversation for Grandpa. My nine-year-old spirit ran clear and worry-free once more. That year taught me that a capable woman made all the difference during a season of death.

*****

My mornings ran into afternoons into nights waiting for Dot's radiation sessions, Dot's doctors, Dot's results, Dot's readmittances to the hospital, Dot's releases. My sleep became nothing. My happiness, nothing. Dot's progression toward death became everything.

She grew thinner, balder, and more withdrawn enduring more and more invasive procedures. She said, "If it had to be anyone, I'm glad it's me because I feel like I can take it."

I somehow felt the same. I'd stepped forward and offered more than I consciously intended. It wound up being more than time, gas money, and an arm for her to lean on. It was a test of my own ability to witness her pain without flinching, tearing, or turning away.

My mother spelled me Saturday nights after she got off work. By then, I was numb, beyond tired. I drove home to Tom—the man I'd left three months earlier. He still lived in our house in New York. I had taken a sabbatical, packed my clothes, and moved to a rickety trailer in North

Carolina. Throwing a dying loved one into the equation seemed a cruel trick. I drove back north on I-95 to help when I'd learned of Dot's diagnosis: Stage 4 lung cancer with three more of the six months she'd been given to live. Back to the house with Tom—like I hadn't already shredded my heart bloody as calf's liver to leave him.

Late Saturday nights, after I'd put the baby to bed, Tom and I sat at the kitchen table as we'd done for a dozen years. He'd crack open two beers and hand me one. Miles away from the need to keep a strong face, tears would come. I wept over and over, and over again, "This is just so hard. I'm just watching her slip away." I drank and cried until my body and mind could focus on something other than the protocols of death.

For those two days off, I lived by the words of my oldest and dearest friend, "The best thing about the first beer is knowing there's another one coming right behind it." And, in spite of our recent demise, Tom's familiar, solid company, helped me stay afloat until Monday morning—buoyant with beer and reassured somehow that I was tough enough to do whatever would need doing when I went back to my deathwatch.

Dot and I sat waiting for her radiation treatment when she said, "I would've done so many things different if I'd known better. So many things I cared about didn't turn out to mean a thing."

I set those soul-deep words aside for when I had the leisure of pondering. At the time, my mind was used up listening brain-ache hard to understand procedures and next steps, medicine protocols, appointments, and navigating the wings of a sprawling Bronx hospital.

The week before she died, Dot grew more fragile and disoriented. She gave up talking and eating, and I couldn't leave the house. The hospice nurse showed up for the first time fifteen minutes before Dot died and, together, we watched her slip away.

Dot's death calmed my pounding heart. She had endured burned skin, a ravaged body, and holes drilled through her back to drain her lungs. I had lost all semblances of order and grounding. We were free.

*****

Ten years later, I'd long left New York and made my home in North Carolina. I sat with my uncle, Ander, struggling for something to say. We had next to nothing in common—beyond our Belcher blood. Uncle Ander loved the law he'd practiced all his adult life, politics, and basketball. I loved none of these. He was my uncle, my mother's older brother. He was dying.

Uncle Ander had oxygen, yet throughout the day, he removed it and crept to the garage to enjoy smokes in spite of his lung cancer. He'd been given six months to live, and he had no intention of sacrificing cigarettes. But even with the smoking, he turned those six months into eighteen.

I loved him in the way my mother taught me to—not with words, but with deeds. We don't coo and cuddle. We make stews, cart people to the hospital, bring groceries, and wipe an ass if we absolutely must.

I sped back and forth on the beltline and I-40 to get to where he lived with his elderly wife in Durham. There is no harder departure than from a house buckling beneath undone tasks. Unchanged bedding, unfolded laundry, unwashed dishes, uncooked meals, unfilled prescriptions. I stepped into that house knowing that my self would disappear so death's process could have its way.

While I worked, wife-d, and mothered, in the back of my mind, I was always concocting ways to ease Uncle Ander's load and soothe his soul: Make neck bone stew. Ask my husband to watch the game with him. Move Christmas dinner to their house. Buy him a basketball history book.

Uncle Ander moved to a hospice home on a beautiful, balmy, fall day. When I die, I hope I am fortunate enough to be in such a place. His struggle to breathe was over, and his breaths were so faint I thought he'd crossed over. I felt blissful to be a comfort to him, even though he barely acknowledged my presence. When the nurse came in, he asked to be wheeled out to smoke. His bidding was done. I sat beside him as he looked at a field of swaying ornamental grasses, a small still lake, and all was peace.

*****

After a long day of caretaking, I'd often drive home feeling lonely and overwhelmed, nerves frazzled, my own needs unmet. I'd question others' gall to keep living as if a loved one wasn't dying. Then I'd remember that judgment is the ugliest part of living, and I, too, had fallen short in so many ways. I'd leave such questions unanswered and keep going.

Years later, I've had time to process these and other deaths in which I've been intimately involved. I now realize something about people like me, my mother, and so many others who have announced themselves at the doors of loved ones when death has taken up residence. The atmosphere seduces us. We willingly plunge ourselves into its unrelenting grip and endure. It is neither gift nor burden. It is simply our way. It's something we wouldn't do differently even if given another chance. Something always worth it in the long run, that always turns out to mean quite a bit.

Afterword

I have always been a keeper of stories—though never a storyteller myself and never a collector of written stories.

It was not my plan to collect death and dying stories. This project had a life of its own. It surprised me how quickly it proceeded; how some stories came forward sooner than others; and how some stories were not ready to be written yet.

As I moved the stories forward, read them, and finished writing and editing this anthology, I gained deep clarity about how storytelling connects us with each other. Through this process I have welcomed back my own storyteller.

These stories have been my teachers and they inform my work. The bones of these stories support me. The roots of these stories ground me. The branches of these stories expand my vision and connection with spirit.

Grief is not an enemy, it is just another visitor who knocks at our door, sometimes early on in life, sometimes later. All it wants is a place in our heartspace.

Cathy Brooks Edwards

Note to Our Readers

Thank you for reading these stories, sharing them with others, and participating in Death and Cupcakes, and Tending to the Heart events. Join us in opening our culture's awareness and comfort with dying time. We are all in this together.

If you are moved, please write and let me know.

And if you are ready, inquire about submission guidelines for a future anthology. I'd love to hear from you at listeningtoyoursoul@gmail.com.

All the proceeds from this book go back into the non-profit heart2heart. www.heart2heartnc.com

I hope you are touched and moved by this collection of stories. I invite you to consider a generous donation to heart2heart so we may continue the work of gathering life-affirming dying time stories; participating in death and dying-time-awareness events; workshops; and one-on-one work with individuals and families.

With gratitude and deep love,

Brooksie

Acknowledgments

I wish to thank...

All the contributors for working with me on such a tight timeline for this project, and for trusting me with your sacred experiences;

Anora Sutherland McGaha for helping me shepherd this book to fruition. Her dedication to the integrity of this anthology and faith in me is palpable. She came searching for me over a decade ago with a knowing that I had a story to share;

Frank Phoenix for believing in me and taking a risk;

Hannah Eck for her enthusiasm and courage to enter the heartspace of 19 storytellers with gentle feedback and suggestions;

Andrea Saccone Snyder for sharing her gifts of creative expression and the ability to see the heart as a vessel and then draw it - pure magic;

Camille Armantrout for being a cheerleader, a coach and a gracious first reader;

The second readers:

Anne deBuys for her guiding light from the mountains;

Sheila Fleming for her creative praise and on-going support;

Lauren Hoders for her efficiency in the details, along with her generosity to me, and this movement of bringing death out of the shadows;

Alisa Esposito for her willingness to meet me exactly where I was each step of the way during this crazy project;

Lyle Estill for encouraging me, being a mentor and trusting me with his heartspace;

Tami Schwerin for her courage to lead the way in this grief work and showing us how it is done within community;

*****

Alisa Esposito, her husband, Chris Lucash, and their children, Amie, Noah and Eden for allowing me and my family to plant our roots in their life;

All the Bend folks for welcoming me onto their land with open arms;

Amy Durso for her willingness to explore the outer edges of this death, dying and beyond work with me—helping me birth this vision from the ground up. Our work together continues to blow my mind;

John Westmoreland for his beautiful music that heals the world, and me;

The Seven Sisters for the many years of practicing ritual together;

All my powerful sisters who carry their torches in unity;

Michael and Cynthia Flowers for helping me remember my own mythic stories;

Carey Smith for inspiring me to live deeply in my body;

Lauren Jubelirer for her mentorship in the mystic teachings of the unseen worlds;

Amiel Landor who keeps me anchored through our daily musings;

Nancy Caruthers, my mom, who had the hardest job of all—mothering me;

Richard Edwards, my life partner, for being my knight in shining armor and supporting me while I do my deep healing; and Zoe and Mia, our beautiful girls, for being my biggest teachers in this lifetime.

About the Contributors

Amiel Landor is a trained clairvoyant, spiritual teacher, and tantric bodyworker. She lives in Vermont and travels often. She believes we all carry divine presence within us and that our work is to clear stories and beliefs that stand in the way of our self-love, creativity, and service. She experiences life and death as an intricate dance, and the foundation of transformation. amiellandor.com

Amy Parker is a clinical psychologist, with a private practice in Boston, and a school psychologist/guidance counselor. She works with children, tweens and those who love and teach them, teaching Mindful Self-Compassion and other meditations. She refuels through swimming, meditating, cooking and spending time with her loved ones on a lake in the Adirondacks, and a cove in Maine.

Angela Belcher Epps writes fiction and creative nonfiction. She has been published in national and local magazines, and her short stories are in many anthologies. Her novella, *Salt in the Sugar Bowl*, came out in 2014. She lives with her husband in Raleigh, North Carolina, where she writes, gardens and cooks, feeling the link to her maternal ancestors. angelabelcherepps.com

Barbara Viola Ford is an office manager, gardener, meditation novice, recent devotee of Tai Chi, lover of birds and the outdoors, cat momma, and widow. She and her late husband, Paul, moved to NC in 1993 from NYC with no jobs, because they liked the "vibe" of Chapel Hill. Now, she's trying to write the next chapter of her life, living in Pittsboro, NC, with her cats, Yuri and Trilly.

Camille Armantrout cooks and gardens in rural NC with her husband, confidant, and travel-buddy of 25 years, Bob. She blogs at Plastic Farm Animals. She has essays in *Nature's Healing Spirit: Real Life Stories to Nurture the Soul* and *Once Upon an Expat*; and has published her mother's memoir, *Honey Sandwiches*, and a travelogue about adventures in Ghana. www.troutsfarm.com/PFA

Carol Hewitt doesn't think much about death, but she thinks highly of Brooksie. Consumed with life ~ Carol runs a business with her husband, renowned potter Mark Hewitt, and a non-profit called Slow Money NC that helps local farmers. All with lots of help from dead friends and relatives who are marvelous with finding lost keys and phones, and, pointing out rainbows. slowmoneync.org

Diane Fine is a professor of art at the State University of New York, Plattsburgh, where she teaches printmaking and book arts. Diane's work is represented in The New York Public Library, the Yale University Art Gallery, and the Museum of Modern Art in New York, as well as in private collections. She has been the proprietor of Moonkosh Press since 1985. www.dianefine.com

Dori DeJong is an award-winning author of two southern fiction novels, *Scout's Honor* and *Good Buddy*. Dori is a contributing blogger for the Hope for Widows Foundation; and facilitates her *Grieve the Write Way* grief-writing workshops. She works professionally in the legal field and is a veteran of the United States Army. Dori resides in Raleigh, NC, with her two daughters. DoriAnnDupre.com

Edwin Nothnagel is a husband, father, friend and healer living in Chatham County with his wife of 36 years and their four-legged-friends. He has been on a path of self-discovery for 20 years, transforming his 22-year career as an industrial engineer to a life of service as a healer. His wife and he are leading the way in relationship and health, living through adventure, discovery and fun.

Gary Phillips is the poet laureate of Carrboro, NC. He is a writer, naturalist and entrepreneur who lives in a rammed earth house with his wife Ilana. Gary reads poetry and anthropological science fiction; studies amphibians and was once chair of the Chatham County Board of Commissioners. His book *The Boy The Brave Girls* came out in 2016. westendpoetryfestival.org/gary-phillips

Hannah Eck is a community weaver and storyteller who lives in a multi-generational intentional community in the heart of Chatham County, NC. Hannah works for Abundance NC, a nonprofit centered on building resilient communities. In her free time, you can find her gallivanting through the forest looking for bones or sitting on a friend's porch telling a story.

Jaki Shelton Green is a multi-award-winning poet, activist and educator from central North Carolina. Jaki is the first African American to be appointed North Carolina Poet Laureate; and is among the first recipients of the new Academy of American Poets Laureate Fellowships. Her credits, experience, and activities are extensive, and global. en.wikipedia.org/wiki/Jaki_Shelton_Green

Jennifer Scanlon is a professor of gender, sexuality, and women's studies at Bowdoin College in Maine. She is a historian with a scholarly focus on U.S. women's history. Her most recent book, *Until There is Justice: The Life of Anna Arnold Hedgeman*, is the first biography of this civil rights stalwart. Her previous book was a biography of Helen Gurley Brown. bowdoin.edu/profiles/faculty/jscanlon

Karen Howard is a former attorney who has progressed from drafting legal opinions and pleadings to writing poetry and short stories, as the youngest of her six children prepares to leave the nest. Born in New York and raised in the Bahamas, she has made Chatham County, NC, her home for many years. She currently serves in public office there. abundancenc.org/to-the-girl-i-used-to-be-with-love

Leif Robert Diamant is a licensed psychotherapist who was on the Duke University Medical Center faculty for 10 years. As an ordained interfaith minister, he assists people in grieving, dying, and officiating memorial services and celebrations of life. His lifetime relationship with Nature connects him with the regenerative cycles of birth, life, and death. www.wildearthconsulting.com

Lyle Estill is a writer and author. He has worked in furniture restoration, as a metal studio artist, as a real estate developer, and biodiesel fuel maker. He is the corner office guy at the Fair Game Beverage Company making craft spirits in Pittsboro, NC. Lyle has transitioned from a technology globalist to a sustainability-minded advocate for local economy. linkedin.com/in/lyleestill/

Mike Wiley is a multi-award-winning playwright and actor whose distinctive original works in documentary theatre, film, educational residencies and performances are celebrated in America and abroad. Mike's work includes *The Parchman Hour*, *Dar He: The Story of Emmett Till*, and *Blood Done Sign My Name*. Mike resides in North Carolina. www.mikewileyproductions.com

Sharon Blessum has lived in the conversation of living and dying for 7 decades. She was ordained into the ministry at Union Theological Seminary and evolved into a psychoanalytic psychotherapist, then shamanic practitioner, ceremonial leader and guide. Sharon is an imaginative artist and writer with many books to her name. www.joyfuljewel.com/artists/sharon-blessum-writer

Tami Schwerin is an NC native who thrives on making social change. She is a co-founder of The Plant, an innovative eco-industrial campus; and Abundance NC. Tami is passionate about death literacy and healing our culture's isms. Connecting the magical people in her life is her joy. She has four children and a granddaughter. abundancenc.org/about/the-people-behind-abundance/

About the Editor

Cathy Brooks Edwards has been a professional licensed counselor for over 20 years. Graduating from SUNY Plattsburgh in 1996 with a Masters in Community Counseling, following a BA in Music Performance, she moved to North Carolina to study at The Body Therapy Institute. Cathy completed her death doula certification from Doorway into Light in 2018.

For over 17 years Cathy has worked with people of all ages in her private therapeutic practice, Integrative Intuitive Therapy. www.listeningtoyoursoul.com

She is a hospice volunteer in Chatham County, NC; sanctuary director for Sanctuary at the Burrow—a green burial cemetery in Moncure, NC.

Through her non-profit, heart2heart, Cathy's focus is on death, dying and beyond, with individuals, families and communities. She offers hands-on healing, energy work, body talk practices, gentle guidance, storytelling and healing music.

This anthology is her first book and the first publication by heart2heart.

heart2heart's Founding Story

heart2heart was born through the heart-breaking struggle and death passage of Chris Lucash, endangered red wolf biologist and co-founder of Sparkroot Farm. Chris lived deeply and had an adventurous spirit. He loved vastly, gave all and dedicated his life to the care and repair of this broken world.

Chris was diagnosed with ALS and died in his sleep on June 4, 2016, one year and two days later. Chris's dying time was supported with a variety of holistic modalities which brought him comfort, ease and support—offerings of hands on healing, music, story-telling and gentle guidance—providing him with the safety he needed to fully experience the changes in his body as he died.

I want for my story to contribute to the telling of a shared world of wolves, fathers and children. A world that will no longer be one of fracture, deterioration and extinctions, but of wholeness, health and abundance. If I have to die, let this story be told in hopes that it will provide one seed planted for the growth of a new story, a new culture.

—Chris Lucash

Learn more about Chris's journey by watching *Staring Down Fate*, the award-winning documentary about his life's work with the red wolf recovery program, and his own lived suffering with ALS.

heart2heart's Mission

We support individuals, families and communities as they navigate the living path during the dying time, death and beyond.

We offer a range of affordable, heart-centered alternative services such as hands on healing therapy, energy healing, and live music and sound to reduce pain and create deeper states of relaxation.

We work with participants to develop a plan that sets the stage for physically and emotionally transformative experiences.

www.heart2heartnc.com

heart2heart is generously supported by contributions from the community, which are welcomed throughout the year, and are tax deductible through the fiscal sponsorship by Abundance NC (abundancenc.org), a 501(c) 3, a charitable non-profit, EIN #20-4327530.

Made in the
USA
Columbia, SC

81822185R00157